Year 2

Disciples

reading the bible

Chad J. Pierce

FAITH ALIVE®
Christian Resources

Grand Rapids, Michigan

This study is part of *Disciples,* year 2, a comprehensive multiyear faith formation program for adults. Year 2 studies build on the foundation laid by the studies in year 1.

Year 2 includes the following five-session study guides, which feature five daily readings for each session.

- Prayer
- Reading the Bible
- Worship
- Living in Community
- Overcoming Sin

We welcome your comments. Call us at 1-800-333-8300 or e-mail us at editors@faithaliveresources.org.

Contents

Introduction

One of the most important but often hidden aspects of Jesus' life was that he was steeped in Scripture. It appears that Jesus had it memorized (and he was not the only Rabbi to do so). He quoted it to proclaim his identity, as in the synagogue at Capernaum (Luke 4:1-14-21), to counter his opponents, and even while he hung on the cross. Jesus was not only the fulfillment of the Scriptures, he immersed himself in them.

Disciples are people who follow Jesus, becoming like him in all they think, say, and do. It follows, then, that as disciples we are people of the Book. We are to immerse ourselves in the holy Scriptures.

In conservative and orthodox Jewish synagogues, the books of the Hebrew Bible or Old Testament are printed on scrolls in the original Hebrew. The scroll is usually kept in a special place and covered with a special cloth. When taken out, the scroll is often kissed with reverence.

For Christians, the Bible is not a book to be kept under wraps—it is God's living Word let loose on the world. We don't usually read the Bible in the original languages; in fact we have a dizzying array of Bible versions to choose from, including paraphrases such as *The Living Bible* and *The Message,* which aim to give the Word a contemporary punch. The goal is to get the Word into as many hands as possible. Let people read and interpret it in their own situations. Let the Spirit speak through it!

All this freedom and openness with the Bible has brought it into the everyday lives of countless millions. But Christians are divided on how to read, understand, and interpret the Bible.

It's not enough just to read the Bible. This wonderful, living book is also ancient, complex, difficult, and sometimes even contradictory. While the Holy Spirit certainly blesses God's Word to the simplest reader, it takes some understanding, knowledge, and skill to "correctly handle the word of truth" (2 Tim. 2:15).

These daily readings and small group discussion guides are designed to help you along on the road of understanding, interpreting, and applying the Scriptures in a way that honors the Bible and deepens your faith. It is my hope and prayer that your appetite will be whetted so that, as Jesus' disciple, you will recommit yourself to reading the Bible—faithfully, regularly, knowledgably, and obediently.

The Book That Understands Me

Getting to Know God 1

*"The heavens declare the glory of God; the skies proclaim the work of his hands. . . . The law of the L*ORD *is perfect, reviving the soul. The statutes of the L*ORD *are trustworthy, making wise the simple.*

—Psalm 19:1, 7

How do you get to know someone? How would you get to know me? Well, you can figure out quite a bit about me from the outside. I'm a white male, married. I'm a college professor and I live in Michigan.

We make judgments about people all the time, for good or ill, just on the basis of outward things. But you don't know what I'm really like just from these things.

To really know me, you need to get beyond these outward cues to the real me. I need to reveal myself to you. I need to talk to you, let you know my personal history, my experiences, my feelings, my hopes and fears.

Word Alert

The church has always said that God chooses to reveal himself in two ways. The more outward way is called *general revelation*. We learn about God's greatness and power through his creation ("the heavens declare the glory of God"). The more inward way is called *special revelation*. Special revelation is the intimate and astonishing story of God's eons-long relationship with his creation written in the Bible.

Recently I was invited to a student's art show at Calvin College. I warned her that I was no artist, but I would be honored to see her work. Her drawings and paintings were very good. I could see her skills on display, and something of the themes in her work. But then I listened to this young woman describe the thoughts and emotions that went into each piece of art. As she began to talk, it was as though she was opening her very heart to me. I felt like I really knew her.

How do we get to know God, the all-powerful Being who made everything? In much the same ways as we get to know each other. We know God from the outside by observing his works. God's fingerprints are all over creation. Almost everyone recognizes them. In fact, it's hard to look at the unfathomable reaches of space or the intricacies of a cell without wondering at the greatness, wisdom, and power of the Creator.

But that's not enough. What is God really like?

God opens his heart to us in the Bible. In the Bible we learn not only the power and glory of the creator but the love that refuses to let go of a broken creation. We hear God's voice calling us, warning us, wooing us. We hear the family story of the Father, Son, and Holy Spirit, and their desire to share their love and glory with us.

But the Bible isn't just a story written by God. It's the story of God, the heart of God revealed through the centuries in covenant and law, poetry and prophecy, and in the experiences of wandering nomads like Abraham, kings like David, prophets like Elijah, and preachers like Paul.

Most of all, it's the story of how God came to us, joined our human family, and laid bare his heart at Bethlehem. It's the story of how God's Son let go of everything to rescue us from the power of evil that had overwhelmed us and threatened the whole creation. It's a story whose climax is a bloody cross and an empty tomb.

How do you know God? Look at his artwork: the universe in its vast complexity and the world in its astonishing variety. What a great and glorious God! But if you really want to know the heart of God, read the Book, God's story, that special revelation in which God opens his heart and reveals that it beats with infinite love.

In the next few weeks, we'll be looking at how to read that book. And we'll look forward to getting to know God better.

Think It Over

1. What would you say to someone who said, "I don't need to read the Bible or go to church. I experience God more when I take a walk on a sunny afternoon"?

2. In what ways is this person right? In what ways might he or she be missing the whole story?

In Other Words

"We know [God] by two means:

First, by the creation, preservation, and government of the universe, since that universe is before our eyes like a beautiful book. . . .
Second, he makes himself known to us more openly by his holy
    and divine Word,
as much as we need in this life, for his glory and for the salvation
    of his own."

—Belgic Confession, Article 2

Live It Out

Be attentive today to God's fingerprints in the world around you.
What things "speak" to you about God? Why?

The Greatest Story Ever Told 2

"This is the story of how it all started, of Heaven and Earth when they were created."
—Genesis 2:4, *The Message*

Katherine Paterson, a master storyteller (and author of many books for children) once said that almost all stories come down to three words: home, adventure, home. It makes sense when you think about it—from *Little Red Riding Hood* to *Tom Sawyer*, you can recognize the theme. The final "home" may not be the same place the hero started, but it's often the better place.

You might think there's danger to calling the Bible a story. That's because we usually think of story as fiction, something made up. But a story is much more than that. In telling our stories we tell others who we are. And often we discover ourselves—who we really are—as we tell our stories.

The Bible isn't just any story, it's *the* story. One theologian called it "the true story of the whole world." It's a huge, sprawling narrative, the story of God and the world God made. And it perfectly fits Paterson's story line. It moves from the creation and the Garden of Eden (home), through escapades of human sin and rebellion (adventure), to the new creation and the new Jerusalem (home).

In between the beginning and end the story bustles with all sorts of characters, from Abraham to Ahab, from Jacob to Judas, from Miriam to Mary. It tells how God chooses the little nation of Israel to be the ones through whom the world would come to know him. At its climactic center, God's own Son joins our human family, battles the powers of evil on the cross, and delivers us from the curse of sin and death through his victorious resurrection.

Of course, if you're at all familiar with the Bible, you realize it's more than stories. There are laws and precepts, letters and wise sayings, and all manner of subplots. But all of these reflect on, support, and explain the big story.

Why is it so important for us to realize that the Bible is a story? Since God has purposely given us his Word in the shape of a story, it follows that we need to listen to it as a story.

It's important to read a book in light of what it intends to be. If you're reading an encyclopedia, for example, it's safe to say you're seeking some information. If you're reading a self-help book, it's likely you want some advice on how to deal with your problems.

The Bible is neither. It's not an encyclopedia about God that lists all the great theological doctrines in alphabetical order. We can learn all we need to know about God by reading the Bible, but we will learn by listening to the story, not by grabbing a text here or there. Nor is the Bible a self-help book direct from heaven. We can learn a lot about how to live by reading the Bible, but we will learn by listening to the story. There's no list of rules for every situation we face.

The Bible is a story, *the* story, and the main character of the story is God. Here's how Eugene Peterson, who translated the Bible's

Greek and Hebrew into contemporary English in *The Message*, sees it:

> Scripture . . . does not so much present us with a moral code and tell us, "Live up to this," nor does it set out a system of doctrine and say, "Think like this." The biblical way is to tell a story and invite us, "Live into this—this is what it looks like to be human in this God-made and God-ruled world; this is what is involved in becoming and maturing as a human being. . . ." We are taken seriously just as we are and given a place in his story—for it is, after all, God's story. None of us is the leading character in the story of our lives. God is the larger context and plot in which all our stories find themselves.

Let's face it, plenty of people find the Bible a pretty boring read. But maybe it's because they don't see that it's a grand story. The real adventure, the deepest understanding comes when we find ourselves in that story, with Jacob wrestling God at the brook, or David leering at Bathsheba, or Mary faced with the choice of letting go of her life to flow with the amazing plans of God.

The biggest adventure of all is how our lives and destiny fit the plans and purposes of God, our Creator and Redeemer.

Think It Over

1. How does the idea of the Bible as the one true story change how you might read it?

2. What are some ways we can misunderstand or misinterpret the Bible if we don't recognize it as story?

In Other Words

"We must take the Christian story seriously . . . because it is *true* and tells us truthfully the story of the whole of history, beginning with creation and ending with new creation."

—Craig Bartholomew and Michael Goheen, *The Drama of Scripture*

Live It Out

Read Genesis 12:1-9. Ask yourself how this might fit into Paterson's "home, adventure, home" story line. How does it fit into the Bible's great story of God and his creation? How do you fit into this story?

Inspiration 3

"All Scripture is God-breathed and is useful for teaching, rebuking, correcting and training in righteousness, so that all God's people may be thoroughly equipped for every good work."
—2 Timothy 3:16-17

What makes the Bible different than any other book? Like other books it tells great stories with intriguing plots and an exciting ending. You'll find it at your local bookstore on the shelves next to countless other books. And yet, while we read many different kinds of books, the Bible is the only one we use as a pattern for our lives. Why would we do that?

Because the Bible *is* different—it's the inspired Word of God.

Many religions have their sacred books, and each of them has a story of how that book came to be. Mormons believe that the *Book of Mormon* was written by the prophet Mormon and his son Moroni on gold plates, that it was buried in a mountain and finally revealed to Joseph Smith in 1823. Muslims believe that the *Quran* was given

---

Word Alert

Inspiration is the process by which the Holy Spirit guided the writers of the Bible, assuring the trustworthiness of Scripture. In the Scripture passage above Paul uses the interesting word "God-breathed," which better describes this very intimate and mysterious process.

by Allah to the angel Gabriel, who in turn, spoke the words to the prophet Mohammed.

The Christian Bible came about very differently. It was written by dozens of different people spanning over one thousand years. The Old Testament was written in Hebrew and Aramaic, the New Testament in Greek.

Despite all of the different languages and writers and cultures and historical circumstances, Christians believe that the Bible is one coherent story, and, in the deepest sense, it has one author. The truth of this amazing claim is revealed in the Bible itself.

Inspiration *doesn't* mean God's Spirit whispered every single word into the ear or heart of every Bible writer. It's clear that Scripture was written by real human authors who spoke out of their own experience, their own culture and language, and their own limited understanding.

It also *doesn't* mean that the authors could somehow see or understand things beyond their own time and place. Like the other people of their time, the Old Testament authors understood the world as a flat surface on pillars, with a "firmament" or bowl over it forming the sky.

So it's important for us to read the Bible with its purpose in mind. The Bible intends to teach us about God and his plan of salvation through Jesus Christ. It's not intended to be a textbook of history or science. Thus, when the Bible says that God places the earth on its "pillars" (1 Sam. 2:8, NRSV), it is not an attempt to provide a scientifically reliable explanation for the structure of the universe but rather to teach us that it is God who created the world.

At the same time, the inspiration of the Holy Spirit means that what the Bible's authors wrote was true and reliable. The whole process—from the writing and collecting of texts to the final choosing of what was to be accepted as sacred Scripture—was governed by the Holy Spirit. That's why we call it God's Word.

Here's a comparison that may help us as we think about the Bible. We say in our creeds that Jesus was fully human and fully divine, both God and human at one and the same time. Similarly, the Bible is a book that's both human and divine. It is human in that it was written by real human authors with their own thoughts and language and understanding. It's divine in that these human writings were woven by the Holy Spirit into the one sprawling drama of God's great love.

Think about that. That book on your bedside table or sitting next to you right now contains in its pages the very voice of God. Almighty God, the King of the universe, has spoken to you and me. All we have to do is read and listen. Those who listen for God's voice will hear the ring of truth.

But sometimes we don't hear God's voice very well. So the Holy Spirit continues that work of inspiration by opening our hearts and minds to hear God's voice in Scripture. Jesus promised that the Spirit "will teach you all things and will remind you of everything I have said to you" (John 14:26).

That's why most churches offer a prayer before the Bible is read, asking God's Spirit to open our minds and hearts to his Word. That's a good prayer for us every time we open the Bible.

The Bible is a sacred book. You can read it with confidence that God himself continues to speak words of comfort and correction and hope to us today through his living and breathing Word.

Think It Over

1. What does it mean to you that the Bible is "inspired"?

2. Can you think of some times in which God "spoke" to you in the words of the Bible?

In Other Words

"There are more sure marks of authenticity in the Bible than in any profane history. . . . I have a fundamental belief in the Bible as the Word of God, written by men who were inspired. I study the Bible daily."

—Sir Isaac Newton (1643-1727)

Live It Out

Memorize the first phrase of 2 Timothy 3:16, "All Scripture is God-breathed." How about the whole verse? It's one of the famous "3:16"s of the New Testament. What are some of the others?

Faith and Life 4

"For the word of God is alive and active. Sharper than any double-edged sword, it penetrates even to dividing soul and spirit, joints and marrow; it judges the thoughts and attitudes of the heart."

—Hebrews 4:12

Some days in your life you never forget. Etched into my mind are the day I graduated from Marine Corps boot camp, my wedding day, and the birth dates of my children. Another day I will always remember is the day I became a pastor. I stood in front of the congregation of First Reformed Church in Holland, Michigan, and declared, among other things, that I believed that the Word of God was the only rule of faith and life.

It seems like such a simple phrase . . . "the only rule of faith and life." And yet that little line has changed my life and the lives of Christians around the world.

First, Reformed Christians believe that the Bible is the only *rule of faith*. In other words, Scripture is the only way we can ultimately learn about God. In his Word, God gives us every-thing we need to know about

Word Alert

We usually think of *rules* as a set of directions that govern how to play a game. When we speak of the Bible as a *rule of faith and life,* we mean it more as a ruler, a measure. It's what everything we believe and how we live is measured against.

our God and our salvation. The Bible is the only source for sure and reliable teaching on Christian faith.

Wait a second! If that is true, why are there so many Christian books out there? Why do we listen to sermons? And even more to the point for you right now, why are you reading this book if the Bible is really all you need?

Saying that the Bible is the only rule of faith does not mean that it should be the *only* book you ever read to develop your understanding of your faith. It *does* mean that every book you read and every teaching you hear has to be tested by its faithfulness to Scripture.

Now let's look at the second part of that phrase. Not only is the Bible the only rule of faith, it's also the only *rule of life.* That means God's Word teaches us how to live. Reading Scripture should never be just about increasing our "head knowledge" about God. A true reading of the Bible shows us how to live lives pleasing to God. You cannot read the Bible as God's Word and not be changed.

So as I stood and solemnly said, "The Bible is the only rule of faith and life," I committed to surrendering not only my mind, but every aspect of my life to God as revealed in his Word.

Followers of Jesus who take that seriously are not free, then, to think of God any way we please or to live our lives merely by our own whims and desires. The God we love and serve is the God who reveals himself in the Bible. We're not free to make him into either a benevolent grandfather or a cruel despot.

The laws and principles found in Scripture are meant to govern every waking moment of our lives. By reading the Bible we can find out how to be a good spouse, parent, child, farmer, home-maker, banker, student, or anything else God calls us to be. We are not free to be hateful and bitter when God calls us to love one another. We cannot devote ourselves to the pursuit of pleasure or money when the Bible tells us to worship God alone.

Recently I ate at a seafood restaurant in California. As I entered the front door I was greeted by a large sign: "WARNING: Eating large amounts of fish might lead to unhealthy levels of mercury." Sometimes I wonder if the Bible shouldn't carry such a warning label too: "WARNING: Reading this book will change everything about your life."

The Bible is how God chooses to reveal himself to us, and reading Scripture is one of the primary ways God shapes and molds us into who he wants us to be. As our text says, it penetrates the deepest places of the heart like a sharp knife.

There are lots of books out there to help you figure out how to live. Before you act on their advice, make sure they're based on bedrock principles of the Bible. And as you read the Bible, the Holy Spirit will be there to teach you, comfort you, shape you. I guarantee one thing: you'll never be the same.

Think It Over

1. In what way do you think of the Bible as a ruler with which to measure your faith and life?

2. How might that perspective make a difference?

In Other Words

"You may as well quit reading and hearing the Word of God and give it to the Devil, if you do not desire to live according to it."

—Martin Luther (1483-1546)

Live It Out

Read over the Scripture passage for today slowly at least three times. See if there's a word that really stands out as important for you. What is it, and why do you think it struck you? Begin to simply pray to God in whatever way your meditation on that word leads.

Christh the Center 5

"And beginning with Moses and all the Prophets, [Jesus] explained to them what was said in all the Scriptures concerning himself."

—Luke 24:27

Like all great stories, the great, true story of the Bible has a center, a climax—someone or something that changes everything. In the Bible, that person is Jesus Christ, and the climactic event is his death and resurrection. All of Scripture, from the first word to the last, is united around the theme of God's salvation of his creation through the saving work of Jesus Christ.

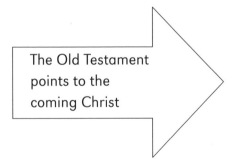

The Old Testament points to the coming Christ

- After Adam and Eve sinned in the garden, God promised a deliverer, who we now know is Christ (Gen. 3:15).

- God called Abraham and Sarah to a new land he would give them and promised that through their descendants (the Israelites) all the families of the earth would be blessed.

- God sent Moses to deliver the people of Israel from slavery in Egypt, made them his people in the wilderness, and brought them into the promised land. The Passover and its lamb became the enduring remembrance of God's deliverance.

- David became king, and God promised that one of David's descendants would rule God's kingdom forever.

- The prophets promised a coming Messiah, an anointed one, who, even in death, would restore Israel's glory and bring a new reign of peace.

The gospels and Acts tell the story of the birth, life, death, resurrection, ascension, and second coming of Jesus Christ.

The gospels, each in their own way, tell us about Jesus and his mission from God.

- They tell us what Jesus did and said to proclaim the kingdom of God.

- They show how Jesus fulfilled many of the prophecies concerning him from the Old Testament.

- They reveal that Jesus is David's son and God's Son, the king who will reign forever.

- Each gospel points to the climax of his suffering and victorious death and resurrection for all of humankind.

- The book of Acts tells the story of the early church spreading the gospel story throughout their neighborhoods and across the Roman Empire. It continues what "Jesus began to do and to teach" (Acts 1:1).

The rest of the New Testament both looks back to the life, death, and resurrection of Christ and forward to his coming again.

The letters of Paul and other apostles, as well as the book of Revelation, reflect on the whole story of God.

- They explain how creation and human life is restored in Christ's redeeming work on the cross.

- They demonstrate how we now live as new people redeemed by Christ.

- They show how the church is the new Israel, called to show the light of God's love to the nations.

- They point with hope to the future when the Lord will return to claim his kingdom.

Over the next couple of weeks we will be studying the different types of literature that make up the books of the Bible. But as you think about history, law, prophecy, gospels, epistles, and even more, do not forget the big picture. You are reading the great true story of the world whose center is Jesus Christ.

Think It Over

1. Think about what the Bible would be like without Christ as the center.

2. Would it still be a story of the whole world?

In Other Words

"In his life, Jesus shows us what salvation looks like: the power of God to heal and to make new is vividly present in all his words and actions. In his death, Jesus accomplishes that salvation: at the cross he wages war against the powers of evil and defeats them. In his resurrection, Jesus opens the door to the new creation—and then *holds that door open* and invites us to join him. . . . In Jesus, the kingdom of God has come!

—Craig Bartholomew and Michael Goheen, *The Drama of Scripture*

Live It Out

Read Isaiah 9:1-7, written 800 years before Christ's birth, through the lens of his coming. Allow its vision of God's just and righteous kingdom to soak into your soul and sustain you as you walk in God's way this week.

The Book That Understands Me
Discussion Guide

In one of the daily readings we thought about the Bible as God's great story that follows the pattern of so many stories: home, adventure, home.

The Bible is God's story, and it follows that same pattern. It begins at home in the Garden, in the fresh dew of creation. The central characters are Adam and Eve, who represent humanity, or, really, all of us.

The adventure begins when they tragically rebel against the Creator-King and are thrust out of the Garden. But God, the real "hero" of the story, won't let his creation be destroyed. And there begins the great adventure, a huge, amazing story, thick with plot and subplots, poetry and history, lessons and letters.

In the middle of the story, the "hero," the King's Son, breaks into the adventure with an act of love and redemption that changes absolutely everything. Finally, the story points toward home—a new home, not a garden but a city, the New Jerusalem.

I say it *points* to home because we're not there yet. We are now characters in the story too. We hear the good news, and God calls us to join in the great adventure of a pilgrimage toward that kingdom home.

John Newton captures something of this grand story and our place in it in his great hymn to God's grace: "Through many dangers, toils, and snares I have already come; 'tis grace hath brought me safe thus far, and grace will lead me home."

For Starters

(15 minutes)

Open by sharing with the group the best book you have ever read. It can be a Christian book, a novel, a book of poetry, or even a comic book. What did you enjoy about the book? Was it just entertaining, or did it speak to you in more profound ways?

Next go around the group and answer these questions:

- Do you have a favorite book of the Bible?

- Have there been any books of the Bible or passages or verses of Scripture that have had a special impact on your life? Why?

Let's Focus

(5 minutes)

Read the introduction to this session (if you haven't already) and then have someone read this focus statement aloud:

The Bible is the story of God's unending love affair with his creation. But it's unlike any other story. In its pages God opens his heart to us. God tells his story, but in words written by human beings like us who were inspired by God's own Spirit so that their writing is utterly reliable and true. It reveals a mighty God, a holy God, a merciful God, a God who is deeply involved in the life of his creation right up to the present moment. The Bible is the great true story of the world in which we live out our own life stories.

In Other Words

"It is clear that there must be difficulties for us in a revelation such as the Bible. If someone were to hand me a book that was as simple to me as the multiplication table, and say, 'This is the Word of God. In it He has revealed His whole will and wisdom,' I would shake my head and say, 'I cannot believe it; that is too easy to be a perfect revelation of infinite wisdom.' There must be, in any complete revelation of God's mind and will and character and being, things hard for the beginner to understand; and the wisest and best of us are but beginners."

—R.A. Torrey, quoted on www.bibleresources.bible.com

Word Search
(20 minutes)

Read the following Bible passages and answer the corresponding questions as time allows, or formulate your own questions:

- Genesis 12:1-5
  This passage marks a new start in God's great adventure story. How does it show that it's God's story?

  How does it reveal the way people (like Abraham and Sarah and us) will be involved in God's story?

  How does it hint at where the story is going?

- Acts 13:15-33
  What do you notice about how Paul tells the story?

  Who's the main actor?

  What's the climax?

- 2 Timothy 3:15-16
  According to Paul, why should we read the Bible?

Various translations use the word "inspired" or "God-breathed" in verse 16. How do you understand that concept?

How would you describe the way it operates in the experience of the authors of Scripture?

Bring It Home
(20 minutes)

Choose *one* of the following options.

Option 1
We've thought about the Bible as the great true story of the world. Using a board or newsprint, **draw a story line indicating with words, or**

better yet symbols or simple drawings, what your group believes are the important events in the story. Take some time to discuss how this story line impacts how you see God's involvement in the world and your life.

Option 2
Discuss the following questions, or decide to talk about a problem or question group members highlighted earlier from the daily readings.

- Christians believe that the Bible is the inspired Word of God. While this is a matter of faith, not proof, what evidence do you find that this is true?

- If God reveals himself in his creation as well as in the story of the Bible, how should Christians look at scientific facts? Does one have precedence over the other?

- What are some of the ways the Bible can be misused if readers fail to see it as the story of God and his creation? How have you seen the Bible misused?

Option 3
Invite members of the group to finish this sentence: "My biggest problem with reading the Bible is . . ." Don't try to solve the problems; just listen to each other. Hopefully, as we go through these sessions, some of these problems will be solved or at least addressed.

Pray It Through
(5-10 minutes)

You are embarking on the huge task of learning how to read and understand the Bible, God's story. You cannot begin, let alone complete, this journey without God's help.

- Offer thanksgiving for the gift of the Bible, remembering some of the things you have learned this week.

- Pray for a spirit of generosity, understanding, and humility as you talk about the Bible together.

- Perhaps members of the group have expressed doubts, reservations, or other problems in reading or understanding Scripture. Pray for each other.

- Pray that your group will be guided by the Holy Spirit, who inspired the Bible, as you begin your journey of discovery together.

- Pray for other matters for which members of the group might desire prayer.

Live It Out

(5-15 minutes a day)

Take some time this week to explore online helps for finding your way around the Bible, such as www.BibleGateway.com or www.crosswalk.com. If you don't have access to a computer, check out a Bible dictionary or Bible encyclopedia from your church library or public library and explore how it might help you read and understand the Bible.

Or, if the whole group agrees to do this, read through the book of Judges over the course of this week. Every day read a chapter or two and write down anything significant you notice, any questions you have, and/or note whatever God is speaking to you as you read. There will be an option in the next session to discuss your findings.

Web Alert

Be sure to check out the participants' section for this session on www.GrowDisciples.org for interesting links and suggestions for readings and activities that will deepen your understanding of the Bible as the greatest story ever told—and as your own story.

Session 2
The Old Testament

Creation and Fall 1

*"In the beginning God created the heavens and
the earth. . . . And God saw that it was good."*
—Genesis 1:1, 10b

Recently I attempted to finish my basement. Not being a handy-man of any sort, I knew this creation was going to take more than six days. I framed, ran electrical wire, took a stab at drywall, and painted. Finally, to my great relief, our recreation room was complete. I sit now in our basement and am happy with my work. But I know there are flaws, some visible, some not. Some boards are crooked, excessive caulk fills the gaps in some corners, and yet I sit there and think, "This is good."

The opening chapters of Genesis tell the story of God, the master builder, creating the whole universe and everything in it. Genesis 1 portrays a powerful God speaking the world into being. In six orderly days, God creates the cosmos and then fills it with his creatures and finally with human beings.

It's a breathtaking story. Imagine nothing—no earth, no sky, no light, not even darkness—nothing. Suddenly the Spirit of God begins to hover over the deep. God takes a deep breath, and never would there be "nothing" again. The voice of God thunders and water appears. Continents form and smash together, creating vast mountain ranges. Birds fill the sky, fish fill the sea, and the earth comes alive with a vast array of animals. It all happens at God's command.

And it's not just the earth either. God continues to speak, and the galaxies, the starry heavens, are formed. Think about it. Astronomers say our galaxy, the Milky Way, contains 200 billion stars. These same scientists estimate that our universe contains at least 150 billion galaxies. And all were formed by God's word.

Some Christians say God started it all in a "Big Bang" millions or billions of years ago, others that the world was created in six twenty-four-hour days. That debate misses the main point of the text. Genesis is not primarily focused on *how* the earth was created but on *who* created it. The point is this: God created all things, and creation was good—very good!

But that's not all Genesis teaches. In the midst of all of the beauty and bounty of the earth and the uncountable number of stars in the heavens, you and I stand at the center of God's creation. The Bible describes how humankind is the pinnacle of creation. Of all God's creatures, only we bear the image of God. We have dominion.

Genesis 2 and 3 tell another story of creation centered in the Garden of Eden. Here we see Adam in paradise. He exercises dominion by naming the animals and discovers his limits in the forbidden "tree of the knowledge of good and evil." He receives the gift of human love and partnership when God creates Eve.

> **Word Alert**
>
> In the ancient world, powerful kings would erect images of themselves in the provinces where they were not often seen in order to claim their *dominion*. That human beings are made in the *image of God* and given dominion over creation means that we are God's representatives to enforce God's claim to dominion. We are stewards of all that God has made; it's our responsibility to develop and care for the earth.

In this story, God is directly involved with Adam and Eve, speaking with them and even walking with them in the garden. But danger also lurks. We meet the snake, who suggests that Adam and Eve can make up their own minds and be like God. And everything falls apart.

But even here there's good news. When Adam and Eve rebel against God and violate the commandment, we'd expect the story to be over. "When you eat of it you will certainly die" (Gen. 2:17). In God's mercy, though, life goes on. God graciously covers Adam and Eve's nakedness with clothes, and while they're evicted from the garden and can never go back, it's not the end of the story. There's a hint of a distant victory when God says to the serpent, "I will put enmity between you and the woman, and between your offspring and hers; he will crush your head, and you will strike his heel" (Gen. 3:15).

God will not give up. He doesn't just walk away from the train wreck of human sin. Rather God calls out to Adam and Eve in the garden. God speaks to Moses and the prophets. God actually comes to earth in the person of Jesus.

These three chapters form the foundation of Scripture. They contain the essential information we need to know about who God is and who we are in relation to God.

God continues to be involved with his creation every moment. And one day God promises to create a new earth with no sin. No pain. No death. One day God will again look upon creation and proclaim, "It is very good."

Think It Over

1. What images come to mind when you picture God as Creator?

2. What do you think it means that human·beings are created in the image of God?

In Other Words

"[T]he minute we start to witness to our faith and to tell *the Christian story* (rather than just our own personal story), we are inevitably driven back to the start of it all: the Creation itself. 'In the beginning, God . . .'"

—Craig Bartholomew and Michael Goheen, *The Drama of Scripture*

Live It Out

Go for a walk. As you do, look around at creation (both nature and people). Reflect on what you see and what that says about God.

Torah 2

"I am the Lord your God, who brought you out of Egypt, out of the land of slavery. You shall have no other gods before me."

—Exodus 20:2-3

The first five books of the Bible are often referred to as the Torah. Jewish tradition holds that these books contain 613 commandments that are to be kept by faithful Jews. Six hundred and thirteen! These rules govern almost every aspect of life: from large ordinances, such as how to worship God, to mundane regulations regarding a trip to the local grocery store or allowable hairstyles.

It's very important to notice the order in which the Torah comes to us. Jews, and later Christians, are given a new way of life because they have been loved and set free by God. Usually when we hear the word "law," a shiver goes up our spine as we are reminded of our own sinfulness. Sometimes anxiety and guilt overwhelm us and we feel undeserving of God's love. Exodus 20:3 makes it clear that

Word Alert

Torah is the Hebrew word for teaching. It encompasses the first five books of the Bible (the "books of Moses"). It contains large sections of law governing every part of Jewish life as well as the story of how God established his people from Abraham to Moses. The laws of the Torah are based on the relationship between God and God's people and are not arbitrary rules.

the law was given *after* God had delivered Israel from slavery in Egypt. "I am the Lord your God who brought you out of Egypt, out of the land of slavery."

So how do we read the Torah as Christians?

The Torah contains many of the most important stories and themes that reverberate right into the New Testament. Let's look at two of them: the stories of Abraham and the Exodus.

The story of Abraham reveals how God begins a plan of salvation for the whole world. God calls Abraham and Sarah to a new land, establishes a new people, and binds them to himself with a covenant. God first speaks that covenant in Genesis 12:2-3: "I will make you into a great nation and I will bless you . . . and all peoples of the earth will be blessed through you." Later God reiterates that covenant: "I will establish my covenant as an everlasting covenant between me and you and your descendants after you for the generations to come, to be your God and the God of your descendants after you" (17:6).

Notice that this covenant is mostly one-sided. It involves God's binding himself to the children of Abraham and their descendants. That's why it's called a *covenant of grace*. Jesus and many of the New Testament writers reflect on this great covenant and its fulfillment in Jesus Christ.

The other great event of the Torah is the Exodus. With Moses as his reluctant agent, God delivers his people from slavery in Egypt and leads them through the wilderness to the Promised Land. The Passover, with its slaughtered lamb, becomes the ongoing remembrance of that deliverance for the people of Israel.

In the New Testament the Exodus becomes the biblical picture of God's final and complete deliverance of his people. Jesus gathers his disciples for a Passover meal (the Last Supper) and tells them to eat his body and blood as they ate the lamb at Passover. God's people today are part of a new exodus. We've been delivered by Jesus' death and resurrection from our slavery to sin and death, and we're on our way through the wilderness of this world to the Promised Land—a renewed creation.

The Jewish Torah is also our Torah. It tells the primary stories that define who we are and the covenant-making, slavery-smashing God to whom we belong.

What about all the laws of Exodus, Leviticus, and Deuteronomy? It's true that some of the laws are superseded in the New Covenant established in Christ—clean and unclean animals, for example, or kosher food (see Acts 10:9-23). Still, even the arcane rituals that were part of the whole system of sacrifices described in Leviticus can help us to understand the atoning sacrifice of Christ.

The book of Hebrews especially shows how Jesus wonderfully fulfills the Day of Atonement described in Leviticus 16. Jesus ascends into heaven to make an offering for sins once and for all—not with the blood of bulls and goats but with his own precious blood (Heb. 10:1-10).

The Torah, the story of God's saving work through the covenant with Abraham and the story of God delivering his people from slavery through Moses, is also our story. When Jesus talked about the laws of the Torah, he said, "Do not think that I have come to abolish the Law or the Prophets . . . but to fulfill them" (Matt. 5:17). He goes on to show that all these laws are summed up in the double commandment to love God above all and our neighbor as ourselves (Mark 12:30-31).

Think It Over

Try to imagine what Christianity would look like without the Torah as a foundation. What would be missing?

In Other Words

"It is always rewarding in using the Old Testament to understand the story of Israel as the story of our lives. Israel . . . was on a journey between her redemption out of slavery in Egypt and her entrance into the Promised Land. . . . In many respects, you and I are on the same journey, traveling between the time of our redemption by the cross of Christ and the time of our entrance into the kingdom of God. . . ."

—Elizabeth Achtemeier, in *The Lectionary Commentary*, Roger Van Harn, editor

Live It Out

Read Leviticus 16 and try to see all the connections there with Christ.

Kings and Kingdom 3

> *"Your [King David's] house and your kingdom will endure forever before me; your throne will be established forever."*
>
> —2 Samuel 7:16

If the Old Testament were to be made into a movie, it would undoubtedly be rated "R" for graphic violence, sex, and language (you have to be able to read the original Hebrew for that). For pure entertainment and gut-wrenching drama, you can't beat the stories of Samson, Jepthah, Saul, David, Jezebel and Ahab.

But what purpose do they serve? How do we read them as part of the great true story of God and creation?

The book of Judges tells the story of how the Israelites settled into the Promised Land. It's not a "happily ever after" story. There's a recurrent pattern (see sidebar) in which the people fall into disobedience and idolatry, God rescues them, and they fall again.

The Pattern in Judges

1. Israel sins against God.
2. God punishes Israel (often by sending a foreign invader).
3. Israel repents.
4. God raises up a military hero called a judge.
5. The judge is empowered by the Holy Spirit.
6. Israel defeats its enemies.
7. There is peace in the land for a number of years.
8. After the judge dies, Israel sins and the cycle begins again.

But with the opening of the book of Samuel, a new era begins. Starting with Saul, Israel is ruled by kings, the greatest of whom was King David. Most of the historical books are devoted to telling the stories of David and his descendants.

How does all this sometimes-despicable history fit into the Bible? By introducing a new and important theme—*king and kingdom*—that echoes through the Bible all the way to the book of Revelation. God, who is King of all the earth, appointed humankind to rule on his behalf, pointing to his ultimate kingship.

David is that kind of king. He wasn't perfect by any means, but he was "a man after God's own heart" who exemplified more than most people a vibrant, wholehearted, passionate humanity that God loved.

At the heart of the story, God promises that David's descendant would sit on his throne forever (2 Sam. 7:11-16; Ps. 132:11-12). The promise is not unconditional: disobedient descendants will be punished. Even so, says God, "Your house and your kingdom will endure forever before me" (2 Sam. 7:16).

Once you hear that great promise, the rest of the Old Testament history falls into place. Some of David's descendants are faithful to God; most are not. God withholds punishment for hundreds of years, but at long last judgment falls. The northern kingdom of Israel is carried away into captivity and lost forever. The southern kingdom of Judah is also taken captive, but is brought back to the land after seventy years.

Here's the message: the kings of Israel cannot live up to their calling, not even David. Despite this failure is the promise and hope that there will be a greater son of David, a messianic King who will keep covenant with God and lead God's people into a new era of freedom and peace.

Now flash forward. The angel Gabriel says to Mary, "You will conceive and give birth to a son. . . . The Lord God will give him the throne of his father David, and he will reign over the house of Jacob forever; his kingdom will never end" (Luke 1:31-33). Here is the long-awaited son of David—a real, passionate, godly, glorious human being.

Flash forward once again. Jesus enters Jerusalem for the last time riding on a lowly donkey. The crowds go crazy. They shout, "Blessed is the king who comes in the name of the Lord!" (19:38). Jesus enters Jerusalem as David's son, but the true nature of his kingship only comes into focus a few days later as he hangs limp from a cross on which is written, "King of the Jews."

Flash forward one final time. In John's great vision called Revelation, he sees the climax of history. Who should appear but the King! "Before me was a white horse, whose rider is called Faithful and True. . . . On his robe and on his thigh he has this name written: KING OF KINGS AND LORD OF LORDS" (Rev. 19:11, 16).

It's all about Jesus. All that history, all those kings, good and bad, eventually comes down to the One who is King of kings and Lord of lords. David's son is victorious over sin and death, and his kingdom shall have no end.

Think It Over

Think about what you know about David and his life. What makes him such a compelling example of human life at its best (and worst)?

In Other Words

"The David story anticipates the Jesus story. The Jesus story presupposes the David story. . . . If we're going to get the most out of the Jesus story, we'll want first to soak our imaginations in the David story."

—Eugene Peterson, *Leap Over a Wall*

Live It Out

Find a book or go online and find a timetable of the history of Israel. Check out not only the biblical figures and events, but also what was going on in the rest of the world at that time.

Wisdom 4

"The fear of the LORD is the beginning of wisdom; all who follow his precepts have good understanding."

—Psalm 111: 10

I remember sitting with a mom and dad in a courthouse in Michigan, watching and listening as a judge sentenced their son to two years in jail. As parents often do, they immediately blamed themselves. They took me down memory lane . . . to a young boy attending Sunday school and Boy Scouts. They told me stories of a Christian family doing the best they could to raise their son.

> ## A Word to the Wise
>
> **We're including the Psalms in wisdom writings here, but it's also important to consider them as prayer. For that you can check out *Prayer*, one of the studies in *Disciples*, year 2. You'll find a whole session and five daily readings on the Psalms as prayer.**

Finally, the father asked me about God's Word. He told me that he had read the Bible from cover to cover many times. Then he quoted the proverb "Start children off on the way they should go, and even when they are old they will not turn from it" (Prov. 22:6).

How could it be true? He and his wife had raised their son in a Christian home, with Christian values and instruction, and he had departed from it, turning from God to all sorts of other things to fill his void.

I told the father that he was indeed a good parent. I also told him that his son was not a bad person but had simply made some poor but forgivable decisions. I reassured him of God's love for his son and for his entire family.

This father is not the only one to raise questions about God's promises in the Bible. Many people can testify, "God's Word says one thing, but I've experienced a different reality." You may have had such an experience yourself.

The third section of the Old Testament is called the writings. It is a kind of "catch-all" for the later works of the Old Testament that do not fit within the Law or the Prophets. Part of the writings includes Wisdom Literature (Job, Proverbs, and Ecclesiastes). Wisdom literature is pre-Christian Jewish philosophy. In it, the writers give their understanding of how the world works.

Wisdom literature, including the book of Proverbs, was written to give us a general understanding of God and his relationship to the world. Think of it as a series of *observations* of the way things usually work in God's world, not as a series of individual promises or guarantees that always come out exactly the way we want them to.

So, for example, "Start children off on the way they should go . . . and they will not turn from it" does not mean that godly parenting *always* results in obedient and godly children. Similarly, the statement "I was young and now I am old, yet I have never seen the righteous forsaken or their children begging bread" (Ps. 37:25) does not mean that righteous people will never go hungry. History is full of examples of the opposite. It does mean that God takes care of us, and we should trust in him.

Other wisdom literature, such as the book of Job, clearly demonstrates that sometimes bad things do happen to godly people.

On the flip side, God has provided deep wisdom and practical skills for living in this part of his Word. Raising children in God's ways most often does help them live in God's truth and grace. Generous people find joy in giving and help in their own time of need. Lazy people can't reap the rewards of their work. "The fear of the LORD is the beginning of wisdom" (Ps. 111:10).

Think It Over

1. Think of a time when you felt that the promises in God's Word did not come true. Did you blame yourself or God for broken promises?

2. What role does sin play in God's promises contained in Scripture?

In Other Words

"Wisdom is moral and relational skill. Wisdom is the ability to live skillfully in God's world according to the laws and principles God has built into the very structure of things. It's the basic skills of living we can use every day to make our lives productive and happy."

—Anonymous

Live It Out

In the Scripture passage at the beginning of this daily reading, God promises wisdom to those who fear him. This week pray for wisdom for the leaders of your city, state or province, and country.

Prophets 5

*"The word of the LORD came to me saying,
'Before I formed you in the womb I knew you,
before you were born I set you apart; I appointed
you as a prophet to the nations.'"*

—Jeremiah 1:4-5

The prophets of the Old Testament were quirky characters. They've been known to wear funny clothes, marry a prostitute, even walk around without clothes for a number of years! These days we tend to think of prophets as people who can predict the future—something like a godly fortune teller.

In ancient Israel prophets were intermediaries between the people of Israel and God. Their role was to bring the people's concerns to God and then return with God's response. Kings would consult prophets before war; individuals would inquire about children. Prophets were unique not because they could see the future or because they did some odd things, but because they had a special and close relationship with God.

> **Word Alert**
>
> **The Prophets** is also a body of literature in the Old Testament. It consists of the major prophets (Isaiah, Jeremiah, and Ezekiel) and the minor prophets (Hosea, Joel, Amos, Obadiah, Jonah, Micah, Nahum, Habakkuk, Zephaniah, Haggai, Zechariah, and Malachi). The "minor" designation refers to the length of these twelve books, not to their importance.

Another thing to keep in mind when reading the Prophets is that they often spoke in what might be called "hyper-language." "The LORD is coming from his dwelling place. . . . The mountains melt beneath him and the valleys split apart" (Mic. 1:3-4). This is not geological information, but a way of speaking that paints a breathtaking picture of God's power and majesty.

As we read the prophets, it's helpful to use the following three interpretive "lenses":

- **The lens of history.** First try to understand the historical context; in other words, try to figure out the prophet's message for his original audience. Consider Isaiah 7:14, for example: "The virgin [or young woman, see footnote] will conceive and give birth to a son, and will call him Immanuel." We understand this as an important passage referring to Jesus' birth. However, this part of Isaiah was written in roughly 700 B.C., so the first task is to understand what Isaiah was saying to his contemporaries. Who was this child? What was his role? Could it initially have been a prophecy of the birth of the good king Hezekiah? For Isaiah's original audience, a message that said, in effect, "Don't worry, God is going to send Jesus to make things right . . . seven hundred years from now" would not have made sense. Unlike the original audience, our hindsight allows us to see that distant messianic future of Isaiah's prophecy.

- **The lens of Christ.** Even though all prophecy fits its own time and place, many prophecies also refer to Christ . . . his birth, life, suffering, death, and resurrection. Look for hints of the coming Christ. Thus the child in Isaiah 9:6 ("For to us a child is born . . .") was probably someone from Isaiah's day, but at the same time the text also looks ahead to the birth of Christ. The

Three Categories of Prophecy

Pre-Exilic Prophecy

Occasion: Prophets who spoke to the northern kingdom of Israel and the southern kingdom of Judah before they were conquered by the Assyrians and Babylonians respectively.

Message: Repent, Israel! Return to God! If you do not, God will punish you by delivering you into the hands of your enemies.

Examples: Jeremiah and Amos

Exilic Prophecy

Occasion: Prophets who spoke to the southern kingdom of Judah while they were enslaved in Babylon between 586-535 B.C.

Message: Take comfort, Judah! God has heard your cries and he will deliver you. You will return to Jerusalem, and God will send a redeemer.

Examples: Obadiah and Isaiah 40-55

Post-Exilic Prophecy

Occasion: Prophets who spoke to the southern kingdom of Israel after they had returned from Babylonian captivity and were resettled in Jerusalem.

Message: As you rebuild your nation, Judah, do not make the same mistakes again. Recommit yourselves to God and walk in his ways.

Examples: Haggai and Malachi

prophets have two horizons, the immediate and the distant, which they themselves did not fully grasp.

- **The lens of today.** After you have studied the original context of prophecy and looked at the passage through the lens of Christ, try to apply the message of the prophets to your own culture.

While the prophets spoke a variety of messages to different audiences spanning hundreds of years, two major themes can be found throughout prophetic literature. First, the call to worship God alone (to a people who were always falling into idolatry), and second, equally important, the call to take care of the poor (to a people who often failed to do so).

Those twin messages are God's word to us today as much as they were to the people of Israel. Prophets speak the heart of God, and God's heart says "Worship only me" and "Take care of the poor."

Think It Over

Can you think of any people today or in recent history who speak with the voice of the prophets? What makes their voice prophetic?

In Other Words

"Prophecy is the voice that God has lent to the silent agony, a voice to the plundered poor. . . . God is raging in the prophet's words."

—Abraham Joshua Heschel, *The Prophets*

Live It Out

Read Amos 5:21-24. How did this apply to Israel when it was written? How would you apply it to yourself and your church today?

Session 2
The Old Testament
Discussion Guide

This week we talked about the Old Testament. We discovered that the Old Testament is made up of thirty-nine books, including three main sections: the law (Torah), the prophets, and the writings (or wisdom literature). It was written in Hebrew and Aramaic and covers a huge arc of time—from the creation of the world to events that occurred in Israel in roughly 150 B.C.

These books include fascinating historical narratives of courageous and faithful people. They also include descriptions of wars, deceptions, adulterous affairs, murders, and rapes. If the Bible were a movie, some say, it would be rated "R." You wouldn't let your children watch it.

Other sections of the Old Testament contain long lists of rules and regulations, many of which don't seem to apply to us. There are also poems, prophecies, and other writings that give expression to people's prayers, praises, and thoughts about God and the relationship God desires to have with his people.

Yet throughout these diverse and sometimes difficult passages of Scripture, a number of themes continue to emerge: God's care for creation, human sinfulness, and God's redemptive purpose. More important, Christians are able to read the Old Testament through its fulfillment in Christ.

As you discuss the Old Testament, think about these major themes. Think about the stories of God's creation, human sin, and God's salvation. Think about what these passages meant to their original audiences before Christ, and then rethink them in the light of Jesus. We may not always realize it but it's true: the entire Old Testament—including Genesis,

Leviticus, Ruth, Proverbs, and Malachi—points to God's incredible love for the whole world.

For Starters
(10 minutes)

Go around and invite group members to discuss one thought, insight, or question that arose from the daily readings. Don't have a discussion yet, just share.

> **Word Alert**
>
> **Some people feel that the term *Old Testament* is not helpful because it makes it seem that the "old" is left behind by the "new," or is not as relevant. Some prefer the term "First Testament," others "Hebrew Scriptures." If you have time, it may be interesting to explore these issues.**

Let's Focus
(5 minutes)

Read the introduction to this session (if you haven't already) and then have someone read this focus statement aloud:

The Old Testament (old covenant) comprises a wide variety of writings that show how God revealed himself through the people of Israel. Considered sacred Scripture by the Jewish people, it's also an inextricable and foundational part of the Christian Bible. Some have thought it reveals a stern and judgmental God as opposed to the loving Father of the New Testament. The Christian faith has always affirmed that the Bible is one story, revealing one God, the Father of our Lord Jesus Christ. But that revelation is progressive. We see God's character and purpose more and more clearly as we continue through the Bible.

> **Word Alert**
>
> ***Progressive revelation* refers to the way in which God reveals himself in the Bible. The revelation of God in the Old Testament is not full or complete. The more we see as revelation unfolds in the Bible, especially in Jesus Christ, the fuller and better picture we have of God.**

Word Search

(20 minutes)

Read aloud the following Scripture passages and briefly discuss at least some of the questions under each one (or formulate your own questions):

- Psalm 104:1-9, 19-27 (or read the whole psalm in unison if you have time)

  In what ways is this psalm like and unlike the creation story in Genesis 1?

  What picture of the Creator does it give?

- Exodus 20:1-21
  How does the first verse affect the way we read and understand the Ten Commandments?

  Do you see any structure in these commandments?

  Why does God give us rules?

  How do you think the law, especially the Ten Commandments, should function in our lives as disciples?

- 2 Samuel 5:17-25
  Perhaps someone in the group can briefly relate the story of David to this point. What do you make of all the seemingly God-sponsored violence here and elsewhere in the Old Testament in the light of Jesus' teachings?

- How does the idea of "progressive revelation" in the introduction relate to this passage? Jesus is often called the "son of David." In what ways is Jesus like David and unlike him?

  How can this story be misinterpreted?

Bring It Home

(15 minutes)

Choose one of the following options:

Option 1

If your group has decided to read the book of Judges and write down your thoughts and questions (see Option 2, "Live It Out," session 1), **go around the group and discuss your notes based on your reading of Judges.** What insights did you find? Try to answer questions or puzzling readings. Do you see the pattern of Judges in history or in your own lives?

Option 2

Discuss the following questions or a question group members highlighted earlier from the daily readings.

- Invite group members to share an Old Testament story, passage, or book that has come to be meaningful to them, and why.

- Do the same for a passage, story, or book that is least meaningful to you, and tell why.

- Does God seem different to you in the Old Testament than in the New Testament? Why?

- Discuss whether the Old Testament is heard, preached, and sung enough in your church.

Option 3

As a group, **come up with suggestions for making a film based on the Old Testament.** What part of the Old Testament would make the best movie? Outline the plot and scenes this epic might include. What might be an appropriate theme song?

Pray It Through

(10 minutes)

Give opportunity for group members to suggest personal prayer concerns and items for thanksgiving. Also note some of the insights, questions, and struggles that have arisen in the group discussion. Praying "popcorn" style, or in whatever way the group finds comfortable, bring your thanksgiving and petitions to God.

Live It Out

Sometime during this week, carve out an hour or so to **read through the entire letter of Philippians in one sitting.** You will be surprised at how you see and understand it differently by reading it this way instead of in the usual bite-sized pieces.

Or read the "Sermon on the Mount" (Matt. 5-7) every day. Reading it daily will allow some of Jesus' crucial teachings to seep into your soul. Again, take time to reflect, to record any observations, or to ask any questions.

> (Web Alert)
>
> Be sure to check out the participants' section for this session on www.GrowDisciples.org for interesting links and suggestions for readings and activities that will deepen your understanding of the Bible as the greatest story ever told—and as your own story.

Session 3
The New Testament

ic Image of Jesus Christ at Hagia Sophia in Istanbul Turkey. Detail from The Deesis mosaics. These mosaics probably from 1261. They mark the end of 57 years of Roman Catholic use and the return to the Orthodox faith.

Gospel 1

> *"After John was put into prison, Jesus went into Galilee, proclaiming the good news of God. 'The time has come,' he said. 'The kingdom of God has come near. Repent and believe the good news!'"*
>
> —Mark 1:14-15

Some churches include four readings in a worship service: one each from the Old Testament and Psalms, one from the epistles (letters), and one from the gospels. The people stand for the gospel reading.

Having readings from all parts of the Bible says that it's all God's Word. The gesture of standing acknowledges the centrality of the gospels to our faith. The gospels stand at the heart of the Bible because Jesus stands at the heart of the Christian faith. Everything before points to them; everything after reflects back on them.

Most of what we know about Jesus, this utterly unique and fascinating person who changed everything—who he is, what he did and said—comes to us from the gospels. Our every hope is based on

Word Alert

In Greek the word *gospel* is *euangelion*, and means, very simply, good news. You can see it's the word from which we get *evangelist*, someone who tells the good news. Our word *gospel* comes from the old English *godspel* (remember the musical?) which also means good news.

his birth, life, death, resurrection, and ascension. The gospels tell us that Jesus is the Son of God who became human in order to defeat the powers of evil and give us eternal life.

The New Testament contains four gospels: Matthew, Mark, Luke, and John. All four provide their own unique accounts of significant events in the life of Christ. Each gospel writer tells stories about Jesus based on his own impressions in order to teach his audience something important.

Matthew's gospel seeks to unite a church experiencing division between Jews and Gentiles; it highlights Jesus as the expected Messiah who fulfilled prophecy. Mark's gospel gives hope to a suffering or persecuted church by focusing on the suffering and death of Jesus. Luke's gospel stresses the universal nature of the gospel by revealing Jesus as the Savior of the world. All three of them relate many of the same events in Jesus' life. They're called the "synoptic" gospels, roughly meaning that they have a similar viewpoint.

The gospel of John is quite different from the rest. It includes many unique stories about Jesus and primarily focuses on Jesus as the eternal Son of God, calling attention to the deity of Christ more than the other gospels.

Some people look at these differences in the gospels as a problem. They'd prefer to get rid of the discrepancies and tighten up the order, to have one gospel that unfolds Jesus' life in coherent, chronological order. Numerous attempts have been made to harmonize the four into one complete biography of Jesus.

But that's a mistake. Gospels aren't the same as biographies; they're more like testimonies or even sermons. They tell the good news to call people to faith in Jesus. This is not to suggest that the gospels, are sketchy or inaccurate or unreliable. It's exactly the chronological messiness, the marked individuality of the gospels, that give them the ring of truth.

So it's best to read each gospel for its unique message. In that way we get four pictures of Jesus rather than a homogenized blend. Each picture reveals different facets of Christ's glory, different aspects of his life and message.

Someone has said that the gospels are basically accounts of Jesus' passion with a lengthy introduction. That's not much of an exaggeration. Look at all four gospels and you will see that a huge amount of space is given to the last days of Jesus' life. Obviously the really good news is how Jesus died on the cross and rose again to save us all.

The gospels also introduce us to the teachings of Jesus. As Jesus himself said, he came to proclaim the kingdom of God, God's coming reign. Matthew 5-7, often called the Sermon on the Mount, is a good example of some of the most famous and difficult teachings of Jesus. In parables both simple and profound, Jesus pictures the surprising contours of God's kingdom. And in his miracles, Jesus demonstrates how God's kingdom will eradicate suffering.

John summarizes the purpose of the gospels best: "Jesus performed many other signs in the presence of his disciples, which are not recorded in this book. But these things are written that you may believe that Jesus is the Messiah, the Son of God, and that by believing you may have life in his name" (John 20:30-31).

Think It Over

Many Christians have a favorite gospel. What's your favorite, and why?

In Other Words

"The Jesus who emerges [in the gospels] is thoroughly believable as a figure of history, even though the more we look at him, the more we feel . . . that we may be staring into the sun."

—N. T. Wright, *Simply Christian*

Live It Out

The gospels were first heard rather than read (books or scrolls were rare and expensive). Rent *Mark's Gospel* as told by Max McLean (available from Netflix and elsewhere). This shortest gospel comes alive when dramatically recited on stage.

The Rest of the Story 2

"In my former book, Theophilus, I wrote about all that Jesus began to do and to teach until the day he was taken up to heaven. . . ."

—Acts 1:1-2

During the years J. K. Rowling published the seven Harry Potter novels, faithful readers couldn't wait for the story to unfold. Each time the next installment was released, newspapers and television showed people wrapped around city blocks at midnight waiting to buy it. Eager young readers began to devour the story in bookstores and parking lots even before they got home.

Theophilus is some unknown person, probably a Roman, who had received the first volume of Luke's story about Jesus in the gospel of Luke. This true story about the Messiah who was Savior of the world must have captivated his attention. Imagine how eagerly he awaited and quickly devoured the second volume, the book of Acts.

Acts serves a bridge from the gospels to the rest of the New Testament. Notice from the first verse that it's not a new or different story. It's still the story of Jesus. What Jesus *began*, as told in the gospels, he *continues* through the power of the Holy Spirit in the life of the church—right up to today.

Strangely, Acts begins with Christ's ascension into heaven. What, the hero of the story leaves?! There is a promise that he will come back, but there's also the tension of a new burst of gospel power about to explode. And explode it does on Pentecost.

Notice how Luke joins his two books. His story of Jesus' birth in the gospel of Luke features an angel telling Mary that she would have a child, the Son of God, by the power of the Holy Spirit. In the second volume, Acts, there's another angel and another promise. The disciples are to wait for the Holy Spirit to descend on them, and a new birth will take place. On Pentecost the Holy Spirit descends and the church is born as the new Israel, the new people of God.

Luke's point is that the disciples and the early church *continue* what Jesus began to do and to teach. And soon we see it happen. Formerly timid disciples speak with power. People are healed and demons cast out. That's the story of the early church and the ongoing story of the church today.

The largest part of Acts tells the story of a Jewish Pharisee named Saul who was persecuting the early church. While traveling to Damascus to continue his persecution, Saul encountered the risen Christ in a blinding light. In this most amazing conversion, Christ's persecutor became Christ's greatest emissary, establishing churches around the Roman world.

Luke goes on to tell the story of Paul's four missionary journeys. Paul and his companions travel throughout modern-day Turkey and Greece sharing the gospel with Jews and Christians alike in an exciting, sprawling adventure.

But Luke never leaves the main theme of his story. It's still the story of what *Jesus* is doing and teaching. Here are a few examples of how Luke reminds us of that theme:

- After Peter's stirring Pentecost message: "And the Lord added to their number daily those who were being saved" (2:47).

- After Paul's conversion: "Brother Saul, the Lord—Jesus, who appeared to you on the road as you were coming here, has sent me so that you may see again and be filled with the Holy Spirit" (9:17).

- At Antioch: "The Lord's hand was with them, and a great number of people believed and turned to the Lord" (11:21).

- Of Lydia, the first Macedonian convert: "The Lord opened her heart to respond to Paul's message" (16:14).

- In conflict at Corinth: "One night the Lord spoke to Paul in a vision: 'Do not be afraid . . . because I have many people in this city'" (18:9-10).

It's clear that the Lord is continuing his work in and through the church. After Jesus gave his disciples the great commission to go and make disciples of all nations in Matthew 28, he said, "And surely I am with you always, to the very end of the age" (v. 20). That's what we see as the story unfolds in Acts. And that's what we see in the church today.

Think It Over

1. How does Luke's emphasis on the Lord continuing his work through the church fit with various Reformed theological emphases?

2. Do you see your congregation and your own discipleship as a way of continuing what Jesus began? How?

In Other Words

Note: The last word of Acts, while Paul was in prison, is *unhindered.*

"This is a remarkable and memorable last word that Luke uses to characterize Paul, and by extension, the Jesus community. . . . *Unhindered:* content and relaxed, practiced and discerning in living the Jesus life in the Jesus way, living a congruence between the resurrection reality and the means by which we give witness and live obediently in it."

—Eugene Petersen, *Christ Plays in Ten Thousand Places*

Live It Out

During this day keep your mind on this theme of continuation. See if you can discover ways in which you are continuing the Lord's work.

Paul: The Man and His Letters 3

"Paul, an apostle—sent not with a human commission nor by human authority, but by Jesus Christ and God the Father . . . and all the brothers and sisters with me, To the churches in Galatia. . . ."

—Galatians 1:1-2

By all accounts Paul was a hard-driving, cantankerous, near-sighted, physically unattractive, courageous little man. Next to Jesus, no other person has had more of an impact on Christianity than he did. As we saw in the last reading, Acts tells the story of the conversion of this Jewish Pharisee named Saul, later given the Greek name Paul. That dramatic conversion changed Paul from a persecutor of the early church to Christ's greatest emissary, establishing churches around the Roman world.

As captivating as that story is, it misses Paul's greatest contribution to the church and to us. Steeped in the Old Testament Scriptures, Paul was inspired by the Holy Spirit to understand and communicate how Jesus is the center of God's saving work for all creation. Paul brought the church out of the ghetto of its Jewish background and proclaimed a gospel for the whole world.

Here's the strange thing: Paul chose to communicate his transforming understanding of the gospel of Jesus Christ through ordinary letters (also called epistles). These letters weren't intended to be sermons sent by mail. They were real letters to real people like Timothy, Titus, and Philemon, to real places like Corinth, Galatia, Philippi, and Rome. And they dealt with real problems like sex, anger, and greed.

In his letters Paul is more interested in explaining what Jesus' life *means* rather than in talking about the *details* of Jesus' life on earth. In that way the letters form a perfect partnership with the gospels.

Here are some of the great themes you'll find woven through Paul's letters:

1. Christ as the Second Adam

As we saw earlier in this study, Adam was created in the image of God to have dominion on God's behalf over creation. Sin defaced that image. Jesus Christ is the new human, the second Adam. He overcomes Adam's sin through his death and resurrection and restores humanity to its true dignity and calling (Rom. 5:12-21).

For Paul, the death and resurrection of Jesus Christ is the central event in human history. He is the Son of God. His death atoned for human sin. His resurrection conquered death. He alone is the author of salvation. We cannot earn our own salvation, and salvation can be found in no other person than him.

2. The New Creation

Jesus' life, death, and resurrection not only saved humanity from sin, but also ushered in a whole new world. Paul understood the world to be ruled by evil from the time of Adam's sin to the coming of Christ. Jesus inaugurated a new age where sin is ultimately conquered and where Christ reigns as King. While it is obvious that the world isn't yet renewed, Paul looks for Christ to come again and complete the new creation.

3. Union with Christ

Paul teaches that we personally experience this new creation because we are bonded with Christ through the Holy Spirit. In our baptism, God reminds and assures us that all the blessings of Christ's death and resurrection are now ours. God no longer sees us as sinful humans but attributes to us the perfect obedience of Jesus Christ. Paul emphasizes that we now must live out of this new identity and become like Christ in all we do, say, and think.

4. The Body of Christ

If we are united with Christ, we are also members of Christ's body. The body is Paul's unique and powerful image for describing the church. Being a Christian places us in a community, united by faith in Christ and belonging to one another. For Paul, our faith is lived out in the body of Christ as we learn to love and bear with one another. The Holy Spirit gives gifts that allow members of the body to do our work in the church and in the world. The unity of the body of Christ is tested by Paul's insistence that there be no division in the church along the lines of the world—Jew and Gentile, male and female, slave and free.

5. Justification by Grace Through Faith

Most important of all, Paul makes it clear that humans cannot *earn* their salvation through good works. Salvation is a free gift from God received by faith in Jesus. Nothing you do will make God love you any more or less. It's grace—unearned, undeserved—that saves us. Whatever good we do is offered in thankfulness to the One who did it all for us.

In the end, remember that these are letters—letters that deal with deep doctrine and collections for the poor, with moral instruction and congregational fights, all bundled together. One of the difficulties in interpreting them is discerning how to distinguish between time-bound issues such as hair length and the timeless truth of the Lord's Supper in the same chapter (see 1 Cor. 11:13-26). But that's also what makes these letters so real for us. In our lives too, the sublime themes of the gospel rub side by side with the ordinary problems of our lives and communities.

Think It Over

1. Which is your favorite of Paul's letters, and why?

2. Which one do you like least, and why?

3. Which of the themes noted in today's reading do you notice in your favorite letter?

In Other Words

"If we are to understand Paul's teaching in his letters, we must see him first as a missionary whose primary motive is to nourish the churches he has planted so that they become fruitful witnesses to the kingdom."

—Craig G. Bartholomew and Michael W. Goheen, *The Drama of Scripture*

Live It Out

Choose one of the shorter letters, perhaps Ephesians or Philippians. Read it all in one sitting so that you get a feel for Paul's writings as letters.

The Other Letters 4

"*But, dear friends, remember what the apostles of our Lord Jesus foretold. They said to you, 'In the last times there will be scoffers who will follow their own ungodly desires.' These are the people who divide you, who follow mere natural instincts and do not have the Spirit.*"

—Jude 17-19

The general epistles or catholic epistles consist of Hebrews; James; 1 and 2 Peter; 1, 2, and 3 John; and Jude. They are some of the most under-read books of the New Testament.

Even though they're called *general epistles*, these letters deal with *specific* issues facing the church then and now. Both Jude and 2 Peter were written in response to false teachers who were spreading the message that because of the freedom Christians have in Christ, all rules—not just the Mosaic law of the Old Testament but also the teachings of Jesus—are no longer relevant to the church.

According to Jude's opponents, Christians receive the Holy Spirit at

Word Alert

In this case *catholic* means universal and does not refer to the Roman Catholic Church. The catholic epistles are also called general letters because, unlike Paul's letters, they are not addressed to a specific place. Today we might call them "open letters."

their conversion, and that Spirit instructs each individual on what is right and what is wrong. Therefore Jude's opponents would accept no judgments or moral instruction from anyone. Their basic teaching was, "God tells me what's right for me and he tells you what's right for you. We don't impose our morals on you, and you shouldn't impose yours on us." Sound familiar?

Needless to say, this relativism led some in the early church to practice all sorts of immorality, mainly sexual immorality. Some had even gone so far as to turn communion worship services into orgies.

Both Jude and 2 Peter were written to combat such practices. Jude goes through Israel's history and gives at least six examples of Israelites who were chosen by God and yet were punished because of their disobedience to God. Jude's message to the church, then and now, was that even though Christ has died for our sins, we are still called to live godly lives.

Here's a summary of the themes of some of the other letters:

- 1 Peter was written to churches undergoing persecution. Full of comforting words, the letter encourages them to recall Christ's suffering as an example for their faith.

- 1 John emphasizes how loving one another is inextricably bound to loving God.

- James (who may have been Jesus' brother) wrote a letter of practical wisdom covering such varied topics as controlling the tongue and the dangers of wealth. His most important message is how faith and works operate together. "Show me your faith without deeds, and I will show you my faith by what I do" (James 2:18). James's emphasis on good works is the perfect companion to Paul's emphasis on grace.

The book of Hebrews, the most important of the general epistles, is unique. While it closes like a letter, it is more like an extended sermon on Christ as the fulfillment of the Old Testament.

The unknown writer of Hebrews especially emphasizes the real humanity of Christ, without denying that he was the divine Son of God. Christ, who completely shares our humanity in order to break the power of sin and death over us, calls us his brothers and sisters (see Heb. 2:11-15).

To help us understand what Jesus' humanity means, the writer of Hebrews reaches back to the Old Testament, where the High Priest was the intermediary between God and the people. The High Priest offered animal sacrifices for the forgiveness of sins. Jesus, on the other hand, is our perfect High Priest: he *makes* the sacrifice and *is himself* the sacrifice.

Not only that, but in his ascension into heaven Jesus offers his own blood before God in order to cleanse us from sin once and for all. Only the High Priest could enter the Most Holy Place in the Old Testament temple, and only once a year. But now, says the writer of Hebrews, "we have confidence to enter the Most Holy Place by the blood of Jesus" (10:19). Therefore "let us draw near to God with a sincere heart in full assurance of faith" (v. 22).

These letters remind us that we cannot take our salvation for granted. They call us to obedience to Christ. They remind us that God does not exist to meet our needs or to make us happy. Rather, we exist to obey and glorify God. At the same time, it's a new obedience whose source and power is the grace of God offered freely to us in Jesus Christ.

Think It Over

1. Which of the general epistles have you read the most? Which the least?

2. Do you agree that their call to the obedience of faith is especially relevant today?

In Other Words

"No is a freedom word. I don't have to do what either my glands or my culture tell me to do. The judicious, well-placed No frees us from many a blind alley, many a rough detour. . . . The art of saying No sets me free to follow Jesus."

—Eugene H. Peterson, *Subversive Spirituality*

Live It Out

Read the shortest of the general epistles, 2 John, and see if you can recognize some of the themes we've discussed today.

Revelation 5

"Then I saw 'a new heaven and a new earth,'
for the first heaven and the first earth had passed
away, and there was no longer any sea."
—Revelation 21:1

No other book of the Bible has sparked more attention than Revelation. Stories of angelic forces, evil spirits, and cosmic battles have riveted and intrigued people throughout the history of Christianity.

More recently, Revelation has been used as a sort of blueprint for the end of the world. A blockbuster series of best-selling novels and movies picture the horrors of the end times as Christians are whisked away to heaven from suburban homes and flying airplanes, while those "left behind" are plunged into a bloody battle against the forces of the Anti-Christ. Preachers roll out charts of complicated codes in order to predict the return of Christ. So far, none of them have been right.

The vivid images and other-worldly language of the book of Revelation seem strange to us today. But Revelation is one of a large number of apocalyptic works written by Jews and Christians from 300 B.C. to A.D. 100. So when John first penned this vision, its language and symbolism were quite familiar.

Today when Christians read Revelation they often ask, "When will the world end?" But the question the original readers asked was, "Where is God in all our troubles?" Revelation's answer is that God holds all of life and history in his hands.

As a pastor and professor who specializes in apocalyptic literature, I have had the opportunity to read countless books and talk to the world's leading scholars about Revelation. And yet the most profound conversation I had about this book was with an uneducated thirteen-year-old Christian girl from Sudan.

> **Word Alert**
>
> **Apocalyptic** comes from the Greek for revelation. It doesn't necessarily refer to events at the end of the world. Rather it implies that God is revealing something beyond human understanding. We are getting a God's-eye view of history with its own special coded language and strange symbolism.

I was talking to her about the tragedies her country was experiencing. This young girl had seen genocide. She had witnessed relatives die at the hands of government-sponsored terror. She had literally run for her life on a number of occasions. I asked her how she could cope with all this ugliness. She looked at me with her beautiful eyes and said, "Revelation teaches us that one day God will come and make things right."

I told my Sudanese friend that in America, Revelation is often used to scare people into believing in Christ. I told her that popular books and movies have been written to accentuate the final destruction of the world and eternal fire and damnation. She told me that her church looks at the book of Revelation as a source of comfort and hope.

Her view is better!

The early church faced dangers ranging from the cult of imperial worship to full-blown persecution. These early Christians endured hardships many North Americans have never known. As people in the church were passed over for promotions, left out of government, and eventually jailed or killed for their faith, many Christians began to wonder where God was.

Response to Roman persecution was varied. Some Christians abandoned their faith completely. Others began to water down the faith to make it acceptable to the Roman authorities. Many remained faithful to the gospel.

Revelation was written for this persecuted church. Its message was coded because the church was being persecuted by the Roman Empire. What was that message?

- First, *God is still in control.* When God overthrows Babylon (the code word for Rome and its power), the shout goes up, "Hallelujah, for our Lord God Almighty reigns" (19:1-8).

- Second, we live in this sin-ravaged, dangerous world as *people of hope*. Though we can't always see or understand, God reigns right now. Nothing is outside his will and purpose. One day God will come and make things new and right. Evil will be banished and God's people will live with him forever in a new heaven and new earth.

- Finally, Revelation encourages us to *remain true to our faith* because in the end we will be rewarded for our faith. The most powerful symbol in Revelation is "the Lamb who was slaughtered," who now has taken up the reins of history. Jesus Christ, who was tortured and died in the hands of human authorities, now reigns as Lord of lords and King of kings (17:14). He holds in his hands the keys of death and hell (1:18).

So the end of the Bible brings us back to the beginning. Creation will be restored. Heaven and earth will be made new. Sin, pain, and death will be no more. Satan and all the powers of evil will be banished.

Instead of reading Revelation as a mysterious book about how and when the world will end, read it as the comforting and invigorating manifesto of God's final victory.

Think It Over

1. How have you interpreted or heard Revelation interpreted?

2. How have you reacted to reading it or hearing it read?

In Other Words

"The little church in Asia Minor is fighting a minor skirmish in the ongoing cosmic spiritual battle—but they cannot *see* the vast scope of the war between God and Satan. So to these frightened, faithful Christians comes the message of Revelation: *God will triumph. . . .* Jesus is firmly in control of world events."

—Craig G. Bartholomew and Michael Goheen, *The Drama of Scripture*

Live It Out

Read Revelation 1:9-20. Write down all the symbolic pictures and words you find there and try to understand what they mean. It's not as hard as you might think!

The New Testament
Discussion Guide

The New Testament contains the stories of Christ, the church, and hope of the second coming. It covers the time from the birth of Christ (roughly 4 B.C.) up to about A.D. 100 with the incredible spread of the gospel through the Roman Empire.

While no one section of the Bible is more important than another, the New Testament in general, and the gospels in particular, tell the central story of our salvation.

The gospels tell the story of Jesus Christ. In them God reveals his love for you and me by sending his Son Jesus to die on the cross for our sins. He also demonstrates his power over death through Christ's resurrection. In them Jesus also teaches us how to live.

The books of Acts and Paul's letters introduce us to the early church and its struggle to exist in hostile environments. They tell stories of bold and godly men and women who risked everything for the sake of the gospel. They also contain the core teachings of the early church that continue to serve as the measuring stick for the theology of the church today.

And they tell us the story that shook the world and established the dividing line of history. God invaded our world, our time, our history, in Jesus the Christ. Nothing can ever be the same. I pray that you read these books and become forever changed.

For Starters

(10 minutes)

Go around and allow each person to share one helpful thought, inspirational insight, or question from the daily readings. Don't have a discussion yet, just listen as people share their thoughts.

Let's Focus

(5 minutes)

Read the introduction to this session (if you haven't already done so) and then have someone read this focus statement aloud:

The New Testament (new covenant) fulfills and completes the Old Testament. This new covenant was promised already in the old covenant (Jer. 31:31-33), and it's specifically fulfilled by Jesus' words and actions at the Last Supper. "This cup is the new covenant in my blood . . ." (Luke 22:20). The blood is Jesus' blood shed on the cross, remembered and received in the cup of communion.

Jesus is the new Israel, the covenant-keeping Son of God. The law, the prophets, and Israel's history all point to him. In the New Testament we see the life, death, and resurrection of the Son of God from four perspectives. Paul and others unfold the meaning of Christ's salvation in the epistles. Revelation dramatically points us through the haze of history to the final victory of God and the new creation.

Word Search

(20 minutes)

Read aloud the following Scripture passages and briefly discuss at least some of the questions under each one (or formulate your own questions).

- Luke 1:1-4
  This is the only gospel with an introduction to the recipient.
  What does this introduction say about how the gospel was written
  and why?

- 1 Corinthians 14:26-40
  Paul is dealing here with a specific situation in the church at Corinth.
  Is his teaching all equally authoritative today?

  If not, what parts of what he says relate to this situation only, and
  what parts are universal in their teaching?

  How do we decide the difference? (This is not the time to debate the
  place of women in the church, but to struggle with some principles of
  interpretation.)

- Revelation 1:9-20
  Discuss the ways in which this opening scene of John's vision tells us
  how we are to read and understand the book. For example, what does
  John's situation signal about the context and purpose?

  What impression does this vision of Christ give, and how might it
  affect the original readers?

Bring It Home
(15 minutes)

Choose *one* of these options:

Option 1
**Work together as a group to compose a short "Epistle to Your
Church"** from Paul, loosely based on the biblical epistles. Write out a
brief salutation (Check out 1 Cor. 1:1-3 as an example, but don't copy it.)
Then write a one-paragraph body, addressing an issue or problem in the
church. Close with a brief conclusion in the spirit of 2 Cor. 13:11).

Option 2

Discuss *some* of these questions as time allows, or discuss a problem or question group members highlighted earlier from the daily readings.

- What do you think are the plusses and minuses of having four unique gospels?

- What is your favorite epistle, and why? What about your least favorite?

- What do you think is the purpose of the book of Revelation? Has your understanding of it changed? Do you find Revelation personally important and helpful for your faith? Why or why not?

Option 3

Look up the familiar birth stories of Jesus in Matthew 1-2:10 and Luke 1:26-38; 2:1-15. On a board or newsprint create two columns and work together as a group to identify the similarities and differences. After you've completed the list, discuss why you think each gospel writer told it the way he did. Who are the main characters in each gospel, and why? How is the situation of the recipients and the theme of the whole gospel reflected in this part? *Hint:* Matthew was written to a largely Jewish audience and Luke to a Gentile audience.

Pray It Through

(10 minutes)

Allow time for group members to suggest their personal prayer concerns and items for thanksgiving. Invite group members to give thanks to God for the particular gift of each section of the New Testament: gospels, epistles, and Revelation. Also pray for each other regarding whatever problems or issues have been expressed in reading or understanding the New Testament.

Live It Out

Over the next week read one chapter of James every day. Again jot down all of your thoughts, insights, and questions. Pay particular attention to any reference James makes concerning the rich, poor, mighty, and humble. Remember that James is likely Jesus' brother. Can you hear any of Jesus in his brother's words?

Through the years many Christians have found it to be a very helpful practice to memorize portions of the Bible. I know some who have whole books memorized. They testify that the Spirit brings these words to mind at just the right moments. Memorize John 1:1-18; Romans 5:1-11; or Revelation 21:1-5.

(Web Alert)

Be sure to check out the participants' section for this session on www.GrowDisciples.org for interesting links and suggestions for readings and activities that will deepen your understanding of the New Testament.

Great Themes of the Bible

Trinity 1

> *"Then God said, 'Let us make human beings in our image, in our likeness. . . .'"*
> —Genesis 1:26

The Bible tells the great true story of the world. It's the story of God's love from creation to new creation. We've looked at the scope of that story and the variety of books and literature that are used to tell the story.

This week, we will look at the Bible through another lens: its great themes. We've chosen to highlight five of them because these five run like multicolored threads through the whole story, and tracing them reveals the ways and purposes of God. Today's theme is the Trinity.

> (Word Alert)
>
> **A biblical *theme* is like a thread that can be traced through a tapestry or a plot line that can be traced through a story. Recognizing these themes helps us to read the Bible with more depth and understanding.**

Where does the "us" in the Scripture passage above come from? The word for God in this verse is *Elohim*, a common word for God in the Old Testament, and a *plural* noun. As you continue to read through the Bible, you will keep bumping into this strange truth: God is plural and God is singular at the same time.

This makes no sense from a logical perspective, and it certainly was problematic for the Jews as well as for Muslims. The Jewish theological mantra, recited every day by pious Jews, was, "Hear, O Israel: The Lord our God, the Lord is one" (Deut. 6:4). And Christians do not deny that for a second.

The concept of the Trinity, of God being one and three, is never overtly mentioned in Scripture, but hints of it are woven throughout the Bible. And the more we see God revealed in the pages of the Bible, the more it dawns on us that God is Father, Son, and Holy Spirit.

Right away in Genesis 1:1 the Spirit of God is said to be hovering over the deep. Later, John's gospel also describes Jesus as being involved in the creation. While the rest of the Old Testament speaks of God as "the Lord" or "the Lord God," we often associate this God with the Father. However, the other members of the Trinity can be found throughout many Old Testament stories.

The Old Testament often talks about the Spirit of God in the law, prophets, and writings. And while the Holy Spirit was available to all people after Pentecost, the Old Testament tells of God filling certain people—including many of the judges, prophets, and kings (see Ex. 35:31; 1 Sam. 16:13; Isa. 61:1)—with his Spirit to enable them to accomplish specific things.

Similarly, Jesus, as promised Messiah and as Son of God, is also present in various sections of the Old Testament. The prophets spoke about his coming, and the books of Ezekiel and Daniel prophesied about him as the Son of Man.

In the New Testament, however, we meet the three-personed God on nearly every page. From Jesus' baptism (Matt. 3:16-17) to his great commission (Matt. 28:19-20), God reveals himself as a divine community of persons.

I love the way Jesus expresses the life of the divine trinitarian community: "All that belongs to the Father is mine. That is why I said the Spirit will receive from me what he will make known to you" (John 16:15).

While the Bible distinguishes the three persons of the Trinity, all of them belong equally and fully to the Godhead. Father, Son, and Spirit are all involved with creation. Together they bring about our salvation. All three created you, all three love you, all three saved you, and all three desire to spend eternity with you.

The best way to approach the mystery of the Trinity is to take our cue from the Bible itself. Rather than try to explain it, the Bible describes the relationship, as in Jesus' prayer to the Father in John 17: "I pray also for those who will believe in me through their message, that all of them may be one, Father, just as you are in me and I am in you" (vv. 20-21).

God is a divine community, a circle of love and unity—Father, Son, and Holy Spirit. And we are called not only to believe in God but to become participants in that circle of love.

You can't read and understand the Bible without rejoicing in its clear presentation of the mystery of the Trinity. The more we grasp this mysterious truth, even though our minds cannot comprehend it, the more the Bible will come alive for us.

Think It Over

1. What is the most helpful image of the Trinity for you: a triangle, a dance, a circle, or a family?

2. What other ways can you think of to describe the Trinity?

In Other Words

"The mystery of the Trinity is not a mathematical mystery. . . . The mystery of our God is not how we can call one three. . . . The mystery is how the Father and the Son and the Holy Spirit can be so united, so much a part of the same mission, so much in fellowship together, that we call them one God. That's the mystery."

—James R. Van Tholen, *Where All Hope Lies*

Live It Out

Read Ephesians 1:3-14. How do the three persons of the Trinity operate on our behalf in this passage? Use this passage this week for your "praise of his glory"!

Covenant 2

"I will establish my covenant as an everlasting covenant between me and you and your descendants after you for the generations to come, to be your God and the God of your descendants after you."

—Genesis 17:7

As a minister, I have presided over dozens of weddings—each unique, each special in its own way. But all these weddings had at least one thing in common: each included an exchange of vows. Although no two sets of vows were the same, every bride and groom made promises to each other. These promises were the foundation of their marriage.

During counseling I always explain to the couple that they are entering a covenant relationship. I reassure them that their relationship will remain secure through the peaks and valleys they are bound to experience as long as they keep the promises they make to each other—and as long as they are willing to forgive each other when they fail to live up to these promises.

Throughout Scripture God makes covenants with people. It's not enough for God to "have a relationship" with people. Like a marriage, God wants to bind himself to his people through covenant. This is a remarkable thing. That God chooses to *legally* bind himself to his people by a covenant is an act of grace. Just think: God wants to bind himself to sinful people with promises of love and fidelity!

In Genesis God made a covenant with Noah not to destroy the earth again with a flood. Many years later, God promised Abraham that through his descendants God would bless the whole

Word Alert

Covenant is a *bond,* an *alliance,* an *agreement,* a *pact,* a *contract.* Its essential purpose is *union* between God and humanity. God offers us partnership with himself. This union and partnership is based on a binding *legal* contract.

world. At Mount Sinai, God again established a covenant with Israel (the Mosaic covenant). While earlier covenants required nothing from the Israelites, the Mosaic covenant established rules for Israel to follow in order to keep their end of the bargain.

One striking example comes when Israel renewed their covenant with God after their idolatry at Mount Sinai. In a dramatic scene, Moses takes a bowl of sacrificed blood and splashes half on the Book of the Covenant, which he then reads to the people. The rest he splashes on the people as they solemnly promise, "We will do everything the Lord has said; we will obey" (Ex. 24:7). But they break their promise again and again. Israel's history is a litany of failure to keep covenant with their gracious God.

The book of Hosea gives as a poignant picture of God and his covenant relationship with Israel. God tells the prophet Hosea to marry Gomer, a prostitute. Not surprisingly, his wife is unfaithful. Then God commands Hosea to search for her and to take her back; a living example of the agony and love of God's faithfulness to his covenant.

Like a good marriage, both parties in the covenant make promises. Throughout Scripture God never breaks promises. God always keeps his word. But Israel does not, and neither do we. We fail God every day. We fail in our covenant responsibilities, and yet God keeps covenant with us. God's covenant is not ultimately based on both sides keeping the deal. It's a covenant of grace—blood-soaked grace.

This brings us to the moment of the *new covenant.* During the Passover meal, Jesus takes the cup of wine and declares, "This cup is the new covenant in my blood" (Luke 22:20). Like the blood splashed on the people when they solemnly promised to obey, Jesus' own blood is now shed as a covenant sign. He is the obedient Son, the covenant-keeping Israelite. His blood, shed on the cross, becomes the "blood of the eternal covenant" (Heb. 13:20), assuring forgiveness for all who trust in him.

One more thing. The new covenant has been extended to all. By choosing a people for himself and making covenant with them, God's desire all along was to extend his covenant to *all* people—Jews and Gentiles, men and women.

As you read all of Scripture, keep the word *covenant* at the forefront of your mind. It's one of the main themes of the greatest story ever told. From beginning to end, the Bible tells how God bound himself with people to fulfill his insatiable desire: "I will be their God, and they will be my people" (Jer. 31:33; Heb. 8:10).

Think It Over

1. How does the principle of covenant unify Scripture for you?

2. How is worship a covenantal act?

3. How is your baptism a covenant?

In Other Words

"The covenant speaks of a deeply personal relationship between God and his people, a relationship so close that God may be thought of as *binding* or tying himself to them, and them to him."

—Craig G. Bartholomew and Michael W. Goheen, *The Drama of Scripture*

Live It Out

John Wesley (founder of the Methodist church) and his followers devised a covenant renewal ceremony, usually celebrated at the new year. Check out the link to it at our website, www.Growdisciples.org. Perhaps your church can plan such a covenant renewal too.

Kingdom 3

"Clap your hands, all you nations; shout to God with cries of joy. For the Lord Most High is awesome, the great King over all the earth."
—Psalm 47:1-2

"Jesus said, 'My kingdom is not of this world. If it were, my servants would fight to prevent my arrest. . . . But now my kingdom is from another place.'"
—John 18:36

When I am teaching a Sunday school class, I often ask, "How many people here believe in the gospel of Jesus Christ?" Usually a large number of hands shoot up. Of course they believe in the gospel.

"Good," I say. "What exactly is the gospel?" I watch as the hands that were raised so high are lowered. Often an individual will finally dare to whisper "good news." "Great!" I respond. "The word *gospel* means good news. Now what exactly is the good news?" Now the room gets really quiet. I press them a little. If they all believe in the gospel, surely they must know what the gospel means.

After a few seconds of awkward silence, someone will say that the good news refers to our salvation through the death and resurrection of Christ. Of course they are correct, but I push them further. "What else is the gospel?"

According to Jesus, the message of the gospel is that the kingdom of God is here. "The time has come. . . . The kingdom of God has come near," are his first words in the gospel of Mark. "Repent and believe the good news!" (1:15).

The kingdom of God is *here!* The good news is not only a future salvation, but the present reality that God, in the person of Jesus Christ, has reestablished his kingdom.

Over and over the Psalms proclaim that God is King. God is King because he created all things. They belong to him. "The earth is the LORD's, and everything in it" (Ps. 24:1). "The LORD Almighty—he is the King of glory" (v. 10).

With the rebellion in the Garden of Eden, humans tried to assume the place that can only belong to God. Tempted to become like God, the stewards of the great King sought to dethrone him. The rest of the Bible tells the story of how God sets about to reclaim his kingship over all.

Christ's coming to earth was the signal that a new age has dawned. God is reestablishing his kingdom. Just as all the world, including creation itself, was tainted with evil, so now all of creation is experiencing God's redemption.

When John the Baptist asks Jesus whether he is the Messiah or not, Jesus responds by describing the social and physical changes that belong to God's reign. The blind see, the lame walk, lepers are cleansed, and poor people hear the good news. Through

Jesus, God the Creator is making the world right once more. God's reign has begun!

When Pilate quizzes Jesus, he seems intrigued with the charge that Jesus is the King of the Jews. Jesus does not deny it, but he tells Pilate that his kingdom is not of this world. But listen to the reason: "If it were, my servants would fight to prevent my arrest."

The kingdom of God is from another place. It's a heavenly kingdom. That doesn't mean it has nothing to do with this world, or that it's only about what happens when we die. It means that God's kingdom operates on an entirely different principle than the kingdoms of this world. It's a kingdom of love and justice, not power and violence.

Enthroned on a cross through an act of self-giving love, absorbing the world's hatred and violence, the King defeats the powers of evil and death.

By his resurrection Jesus reestablishes God's reign. In the words of the eighth-century hymn: "Allelluia! Now we cry to our King immortal, who, triumphant, burst the bars of the tomb's dark portal."

With Jesus' redeeming death and resurrection, all creation is on a journey back to its Creator. The good news of the gospel is that God rules and is restoring his broken creation.

Of course, if you watch the news, it is evident that evil is still present. How can this be if God's kingdom is here? While the Bible teaches that God's kingdom has come in Christ, it will not be fully realized until Christ comes again. On that great day a new creation will see the fullness of God's kingdom.

Until then, Christians live by the contours of the world to come. We live as citizens of the kingdom of God. That's the kingdom where God is worshiped and obeyed, where all people are valued, where creation is cared for, where the poor are fed, where justice and mercy reign. Jesus taught us to pray, "Your kingdom come." That means, "Your will be done, on earth as it is in heaven."

As you read the Bible, you'll recognize the theme of God's kingdom from beginning to end. That theme is at the very heart of the good news.

Think It Over

1. Some people find the biblical idea of God's kingdom out of sync with the democratic age in which we live. How might you respond to them?

2. In what way is this theme helpful in your understanding of God and of your place in the world?

3. What difference does it make to know that God's kingdom is already here, but not yet fully realized? What does that mean for our lives here and now?

In Other Words

"We're not planning the entire kingdom operation, and we're not responsible for its ultimate success. We're just the agents. We have to do our own part the best we can. . . . We use the word *agent* in the sense of *one who acts in the interest of,* but it always makes me think of us more like secret agents. . . . It all seems very sneaky and exciting."

—Debra Rienstra, *So Much More*

Live It Out

In what ways will you be an agent of God's coming kingdom today? Commit yourself to "doing your part" in bringing about that kingdom more fully in your work or at home as a citizen of that kingdom.

Providence 4

*"I am convinced that neither death nor life,
neither angels nor demons, neither the present nor
the future, nor any powers, neither height nor depth,
nor anything else in all creation, will be able to
separate us from the love of God
that is in Christ Jesus our Lord."*

—Romans 8:38-39

One of the most difficult experiences as a parent is losing control of your child. I'm not talking about the teenage years. What I mean is that there are times as a parent when things in your child's life are out of your control.

This past year our three-year-old son had surgery. It was not a major one, but I was still nervous as I looked at my little boy, knowing what was about to happen. On the morning of the surgery, my wife and I drove him to the hospital, and we sat there waiting. As we waited, my nerves began to get the better of me. I paced, I fretted, I worried, and then I prayed.

Soon a nurse came out to the waiting room and gave Michael some medicine to sedate him so that the anesthesia would be less "eventful." Over the next couple of minutes I watched the energy drain from his body until he was limp in our arms. When the time came, the surgeon came out, reassured us that everything would be all right, and then took our son.

That was the hardest part . . . letting go. Yet despite my anxiety, I felt a peace as I watched the doctor carry my son off to the unknown. Somehow I knew that no matter the outcome, things were going to work out. Part of it was because the doctor exuded an aura of competence and compassion. He had done this surgery many times before.

But more important, I knew that God was in control.

God is in control. From beginning to end, Scripture constantly makes this audacious claim and provides startling evidence of its truth. In the Old Testament we see God's providence most clearly in the story of Joseph at the end of Genesis. Chapter after chapter, we follow the convoluted trail of Joseph's troubles. Betrayed by his brothers, enslaved in Egypt, imprisoned by false accusation, forgotten by his friends, Joseph emerges as the pivotal player in God's plan to save his people. In

> **Word Alert**
>
> **God's control is often called *providence*. This doctrine points to the fact that God not only created the world but is constantly involved with it and with us, providing for our needs and bending history to his purposes.**

the end he tells his brothers, "You intended to harm me, but God intended it for good to accomplish what is now being done, the saving of many lives" (Gen. 50:20).

The same theme shines at the heart of the New Testament. Even in the world's darkest moment, when God's own Son hung from a cross, God was in control. As Peter proclaimed to the people of Jerusalem on Pentecost, "[Jesus] was handed over to you by *God's deliberate plan and foreknowledge.* . . . But God raised him from the dead . . . because it is impossible for death to keep its hold on him" (Acts 2:23-24).

If God works his good purposes even through the horror of a cross, then we can trust God to work out his good purposes in our dark moments too.

Still, the presence of evil remains one of the deepest mysteries for Christians and causes many to doubt that God is in control. The suffering and tears, the violence and injustice of our lives and of this world are real. They cannot be brushed away with a text and a smile.

We're in a battle for the world. The powers of evil are real and malignant. There is no guarantee that we will personally emerge from the battle without a scratch. Doubt and fear dog our path.

What we have is the testimony of the Bible that God is King, and he will win the battle. The cross and resurrection of Jesus are the signs of God's ultimate victory.

Despite what may be happening in your life, and despite the chaotic nature of this world, God is in control. All we have to learn is how to let go. Just as I had to hand my son over to someone else for surgery, we need to trust that God's covenant promises will prevail, God's kingdom will triumph, and God's new creation will dawn.

Think It Over

Has your suffering or the suffering of the world caused you to doubt God's goodness? How have you dealt with those doubts?

In Other Words

"Because Jesus suffered death on the cross, then conquered death through resurrection, our suffering too becomes pliable to hope. Our dark caves can begin to crack open and let in that resurrection light."

—Debra Rienstra, *So Much More*

Live It Out

Memorize the words of the text for today. They may come to you in moments when you most need them.

Justice 5

"Suppose a brother or sister is without clothes and daily food. If one of you says to them, 'Go in peace; keep warm and well fed,' but does nothing about their physical needs, what good is it? In the same way, faith by itself, if it is not accompanied by action, is dead."

—James 2:15-17

The sick, the poor, the marginalized, those whom society has often forgotten, have always been close to God's heart. The Bible picks up the rhythm of that heartbeat in its attention to what Jesus called "the least of these." As we have already learned, the message of the prophets, reiterated and exemplified by Jesus Christ, is that God cares about those who suffer. And God expects his followers to do the same.

The prophet Amos prophesied vigorously against Israel in the eighth century B.C. He declared that God was going to destroy them by means of the mighty Assyrian army. One of the primary reasons for God's displeasure with Israel was that they had trampled on the poor. "Hear this word, you cows of Bashan . . . who oppress the poor. . . . The time will surely come when you will be taken away with hooks" (Amos 4:1-2). The luxurious lifestyles of the wealthy few were coming at the expense of the very lives of the poor.

Not even religious devotion could cover this neglect of the poor: "Even though you bring me burnt offerings and grain offerings, I will not accept them. . . . But let justice roll on like a river, righteousness like a never-failing stream!" (5:22-24).

Jesus continued the prophetic message of God's concern for the marginalized. He placed his hands on the untouchable sick. He ate with the outcasts of society: Roman sympathizers, tax collectors, prostitutes, and sinners. He walked with them. He lived with them. He ministered to them.

James, the brother of Jesus, echoes the message of the ascended Christ. In the Scripture passage we've chosen for this reading, James has little use for mere "lip service" toward the suffering and marginalized. Followers of Jesus are called, even commanded, by God to help those who are in need.

God's concern for the marginalized, however, is no blanket condemnation of the wealthy. Scripture is full of examples of God blessing people with great wealth and status: think of Abraham, David, and Solomon, among others. And Jesus' own ministry was funded by wealthy women.

Still, the Bible often warns of the dangers of wealth. Jesus warned the disciples, "It is hard for the rich to enter the kingdom of heaven" (Matt. 19:23). Paul wrote to Timothy, "Command those who are rich in this present world not to be arrogant nor to put their hope in wealth . . . but to put their hope in God" (1 Tim. 6:17).

We live in a society that is consumed with stuff. In the United States, "Black Friday" refers to the day after Thanksgiving when

Christmas shopping pulls stores over the line from debit to profit. It's generally the biggest shopping day of the year.

Let's contrast that with another Friday . . . Good Friday. On this day Jesus committed the ultimate act of unselfishness. He offered himself as a sacrifice for sinful humanity.

Recently I went to a fancy store to buy a ridiculously expensive doll for my daughter. The store was full of people buying dolls, clothes, and accessories. Literally tens of thousands of dollars were spent before my very eyes. Outside the store stood a man with no home, no food. I watched as so many of those people (myself included) who had just paid all this money for dolls simply walked by this man. I'm not judging anyone other than myself, but I wonder what Jesus thinks about a world that spends so much on so little and closes its eyes to the basic needs of a brother or sister.

As you read the Scriptures, take note of the God who turns things upside down. Listen to the song of Mary, whose son, God's Son, was born in a stable and laid in a manger: "My soul glorifies the Lord. . . . He has brought down rulers from their thrones but has lifted up the humble. He has filled the hungry with good things, but has sent the rich away empty" (Luke 1:46, 52-53).

As you read the Scriptures, remember that you are gaining a glimpse of God's heart—a heart that beats with justice and compassion.

Think It Over

1. In what ways does today's church succeed or fail to give proper weight to the biblical theme of justice for the poor and marginalized?

2. How much of a part does justice play in your personal discipleship? Explain.

In Other Words

"Every policy, both public and private, must be measured by its impact on the poor and marginalized because biblical faith teaches that one of the central criterion by which God judges societies is how they treat the least advantaged."

—Ronald J. Sider, *Just Generosity*

Live It Out

Choose one way to obey Jesus' command to help those in need this week. Use your imagination; maybe do a little online research. Will you write letters for Bread for the World? Serve at a soup kitchen? Purchase disposable diapers and personal care products for a women's shelter?

Great Themes of the Bible
Discussion Guide

In the first week of this course on reading the Bible, you were introduced to three themes that are woven throughout Scripture: creation, fall, and redemption.

This week you have been introduced to five other important themes in the Bible: Trinity, covenant, kingdom, providence, and justice. One of the things that convinces us that the Bible is trustworthy is that it tells a consistent story. As we read that story, it's possible to trace certain brightly shining themes through the complexities and particularities of the text.

It's hard to grasp the unity of the Bible if you don't understand and recognize these themes. They're like the rebar in concrete or the frame of a house. They hold it all together.

These themes are not mere human constructs but words and ideas by which God's character and truth are revealed to us.

Remember that our goal is always to understand who God is, what he has done for us, and what he desires from us.

For Starters
(10 minutes)

Go around the group and have each person mention one helpful thought, inspirational insight, or question from the daily readings. Don't have a discussion yet, just listen as everyone shares their own thoughts.

Let's Focus

(5 minutes)

Read the introduction to this session (if you haven't already) and then have someone read this focus statement aloud:

One of the keys to unlocking the Bible for our understanding and interpretation is to grasp its main themes or concepts. In the *Godfather* movies, the themes that weave through the entire saga include greed, love, justice, and loyalty. The story of the whole world told in Scripture also has themes and concepts that are woven into a beautiful tapestry of truth. These themes run through the whole Scripture and are the main concepts or metaphors by which God reveals himself to us.

Word Search

(20 minutes)

Read aloud the following Scripture passages and briefly discuss at least some of the questions under each one (or formulate your own questions).

*   Matthew 3:13-17
    See how many biblical themes you can recognize in this story of Jesus' baptism. (Perhaps there are some you become aware of that were not discussed in the daily readings.) Remember that the concept is there even though the exact word may not be used. For example, pair this reading with Psalm 2:6-7.

*   2 Samuel 7:1-16
    This is the key promise God makes to David—a promise that is echoed through the rest of the Bible and points to Christ. As with the previous text, see how many biblical themes you can recognize in this story. Again, there may be some additional themes not suggested in the daily readings.

Bring It Home
(15 minutes)

Choose one of the following options:

Option 1

As a group work at making a banner on paper that illustrates all the themes discussed this week, along with any others you want to show. You may use words, but also try to express the theme with symbols, metaphors, or simple diagrams or drawings of some kind. Have fun as you grow in your understanding of these themes!

Option 2

Discuss *some* of these questions as time allows, or discuss a problem or question group members highlighted earlier from the daily readings.

- In your own thinking, or in group discussions, what additional biblical themes have you uncovered? Discuss why they are important themes and how they bind the story together.

- Share together how you might use the themes you've discussed as ways of addressing God in prayer. Is it helpful to you to have a larger palette of colorful and meaningful names by which to address God?

- Of the five themes highlighted in this week's daily readings, which is most significant for your faith, and why? How does it function in your life of faith? Which is least significant, and why?

Option 3

Make sure you have hymnals available for everyone in the group. Assign a theme (including ones not discussed in the daily readings) to everyone in the group. **Using the index, or just paging through the hymnals, find hymns or songs that especially highlight that theme.** Share your hymns with each other. Identify your favorite and tell why. If you have time, maybe you can sing a few hymns together.

Pray It Through
(10 minutes)

The Lord's Prayer includes many of the biblical themes we've discussed. Pray the Lord's Prayer together. After each petition, stop and allow group members to add their own thanksgiving or prayers as they recognize some of the themes that describe God's character and purpose. You may also wish to add other petitions suggested by the phrases of the Lord's Prayer that express your personal concerns or those of others.

Live It Out

Choose one of the biblical themes and see how often it's suggested by events in your daily life. Use it as a focus in your prayers. Look for it in worship. Pick up its threads in your regular reading of the Bible.

Web Alert

Be sure to check out the partici-pants' section for this session on www.GrowDisciples.org for inter-esting links and suggestions for readings and activities that will deepen your understanding of the great themes of the Bible.

Session 5
Digging In

reek
lene
unto
tone
ore.

neth
ther

ve taken
he sepul-
where they

forth, and
came to

she w
looke
12
si ng, the
other at
ody of Jes
13 And
weepe
unto them, B
taken away m
not where th
14 And wh
she turned
Jesus sta
it was J
15

Interpreting the Bible 1

> "Rather, we have renounced secret and shameful ways; we do not use deception, nor do we distort the word of God. On the contrary, by setting forth the truth plainly we commend ourselves to everyone's conscience in the sight of God."
>
> —2 Corinthians 4:2

One of my most difficult tasks as a pastor was presiding over the funeral of a sixteen-year-old boy in my congregation who was killed in a freak accident while working on a car. What do you say to comfort a family at a time like that?

During the service I focused on the promises that God made to this young man at his baptism. I encouraged his parents to remember especially in this difficult time, that in baptism God promised to forgive sins, to send the Spirit, and to unite us to Christ in his death and resurrection. God had put his seal on this young boy, and God would not break his promises.

Afterward I went to my office to get ready to go to the cemetery. There I found three people intent on challenging my theology of baptism. Their denomination recognizes only believer's baptism, not infant baptism. I was in no mood for a theological debate, so I told them that while I respected their views on Scripture, their friend who had died was part of a denomination that interprets the Bible differently. They were not satisfied with my answer.

Why are there so many different denominations? There's only one Bible, so why so many different theologies and churches? If everyone just lived according to the Bible, wouldn't all Christians believe the same things?

The problem is that no one can "just read" the Bible. When you read Scripture, you are always interpreting it. Whether your understanding of Scripture is "conservative" or "liberal," figurative or literal, it's all about interpretation. Did God create the universe in six twenty-four-hour days, or are these symbolic numbers that open up to eons? What about the role of women in the church? Homosexuals? What will happen in the end times? Differences of opinion on these issues are not based upon whether or not someone is a Christian, or whether or not she believes the Bible is inspired. Rather they are based on how we read and interpret Scripture.

Think about it. Our world is filled with many nations, peoples, languages, economies, and cultures. Everyone who reads Scripture brings who they are to the text. Try as I might, I cannot read the Bible as someone other than a middle-class white American male. I don't apologize for it; it's how God made me. But not everyone reads the Bible like I do. People around the world from different cultures and different economic backgrounds will interpret Scripture differently. That's OK. In fact, that's how God intended it.

History plays a part too. Roman Catholics use different principles of interpretation than Reformed churches. Pentecostals differ with the Orthodox over the role of the Holy Spirit. In a perfect world we might all agree on everything. But because of sin and confusion, tradition and background, churches interpret Scripture differently.

Even Peter and Paul did not agree on how to interpret the Bible all the time.

A word of warning. I have said that we should respect differences in biblical interpretation among the churches, but I have not said every approach is equally good. We are not allowed to make the Bible say whatever it is we want to say. God has given us guidelines.

As we've walked through the Bible, some principles have emerged already. Pay attention to the kind of literature it is—poetry and wisdom needs to be understood differently than law or command. Read prophecy through both a close-up and a wide-angle lens. Distinguish in Paul's letters between commands that address only immediate situations and those that address all times and places. In the next few days we will look at some more principles.

The heart of good interpretation of Scripture is humility. One day another pastor and I were disagreeing on a topic. He asked me how I could hold my opinion, based upon a number of biblical passages. I told him I agreed that those passages seemed to support his view. Then I asked him about a number of other passages that seemed to contradict his ideas. He responded: "I choose not to read those passages."

Sometimes Scripture doesn't even seem to agree with itself. As sinners we have to admit that we will never know the full truth about God until we see him face to face. Until then, we wrestle to understand God, his Word, and his will for our lives.

I counsel people to be 100 percent committed to their church's theology and their own conscience—but also to be 100 percent open to the idea that they might be wrong. God created you, and everyone else, to engage him in his Word. Read it, study it, interpret it, discuss it, and be changed.

Think It Over

1. Can you think of a time when your interpretation of Scripture differed from someone else's? What was the issue? How was it resolved?

2. If not, what happened to the relationship or community as a result of the disagreement? Would you handle it differently today?

In Other Words

"The Christian community is as concerned with *how* we read the Bible as *that* we read it. It is not sufficient to place a Bible in a person's hands with the command 'Read it.' That is quite as foolish as putting a set of car keys in an adolescent's hands, giving him a Honda, and saying, 'Drive it.'"

—Eugene Peterson, *Eat This Book*

Live It Out

Visit a website like www.crosswalk.com, or www.BibleGateway.com and explore some of the tools for interpretation available.

Scripture Interprets Scripture 2

"Jesus answered . . . 'It is also written:
Do not put the Lord your God to the test.'"
—Matthew 4:7

I love baseball. I like the characters, the rules, and the flow of the game. I like going to the ballpark. I like watching baseball on television and I even listen to games on the radio. Not all my friends share my passion. Some say the game is too long, too slow, too boring. Rather than watch entire games, one friend says he would rather just watch the highlights of the game on sports television. In one minute, he says, he can see all the "good stuff"—by which he means home runs and incredible defensive plays—without having to waste his time with all the boring moments of the game.

That, in a nutshell, is what's wrong with the world today. Nobody watches baseball anymore! What I mean is that nobody wants to invest themselves in anything. They prefer highlights to the actual game. And it's not just baseball either.

We live in a culture of sound bites. Watch television and pay attention to how often the screen or camera angle changes. Television producers understand that people do not have long attention spans.

That's also true when it comes to Scripture interpretation. People want helpful verses, but they do not want to wrestle with all of

Scripture. They'll put Bible verses on T-shirts or on bumper stickers. They'll even paint them on their walls in their homes. They want verses, not Scripture.

Don't get me wrong. I have no problem with having a favorite verse. But this is not the primary way Scripture is supposed to be used. The Bible is not a book of magic sayings to comfort us in times of trouble. The world of biblical interpretation is not the world of sound bites.

As I have noted throughout many of these readings, although Scripture is made up of many different authors and genres, it has one overall message. Certain commands in Scripture, when taken out of context, have had disastrous effects. People have read the Bible to justify everything from slavery to genocide.

Scripture is best understood when it is interpreted by other Scripture. This very old and wise principle was emphasized by John Calvin and other reformers, and by Jesus himself.

Let's look at an example of how that works. The verse printed at the beginning of this daily reading comes from the story of Jesus' temptation by the devil in the wilderness. In many ways, it was a showdown over how to interpret the Bible.

The devil comes to Jesus each time with a temptation to abandon his mission and take the easy way. "Why go hungry—just turn these stones into bread," the devil suggests. Jesus replies with Scripture from Deuteronomy: "It is written: 'People do not live on bread alone, but on every word that comes from the mouth of God'" (Matt. 4:4).

OK, the devil must have thought, *I know some Scripture too.* Taking Jesus to a tower of the temple, he invites Jesus to cast himself down, again, a temptation cloaked in Scripture: "He will command his angels concerning you, and they will lift you up in their hands, so that you will not strike your foot against a stone" (4:6).

Now listen to Jesus' reply. "It is also written: 'Do not put the Lord your God to the test'" (v. 7). Notice that Jesus doesn't say, "Your text doesn't mean that at all." Nor does he say, "It's all a matter of interpretation." He says, "It is also written." He places the devil's crass literalism next to his own careful interpretation.

Jesus knows that Scripture is one whole story, not a series of discrete texts. He interprets Scripture with Scripture.

Even when looking at Scripture as a whole, interpreting the Bible can be a difficult task. But there is no teacher, no pastor, no friend, no one that will help explain a particular Bible passage better than a thorough knowledge of the rest of Scripture.

As you read the Bible you will be amazed at how the parts connect into one theological whole. Let the Word itself be your interpreter and you will have the fullest interpretation of Scripture possible. You will be even more amazed at the God whose heart is revealed throughout the Word.

One of our goals as disciples is to move beyond short verses and pithy Christian sayings, beyond religious posters, bumper stickers, and T-shirts. We have been given the Word of God to read, to digest, to fit together. Quick answers are rarely right and full. So read the Word—all of it—and be amazed.

Think It Over

What are some of the issues your church struggles with today? How might this principle of Scripture interpreting Scripture apply?

In Other Words

"Scripture, Jesus teaches us again and again, is nothing less than God's own words. But precisely because there are many words in the books of Scripture, and because at times they are in tension . . . Jesus teaches us how to move among these words in reverent freedom, giving now this word, now that, the priority."

—Frederick Dale Brunner, *The Christbook*

Live It Out

Read Romans 3:21-31 along with James 2:14-26. What do these passages say? How can you harmonize the two ideas? What difference does it make in how you live today?

Our Divine Guide: The Holy Spirit 3

"But the Advocate, the Holy Spirit, whom the Father will send in my name, will teach you all things and will remind you of everything I have said to you."
—John 14:26

Throughout my school years I had a number of good teachers. Some were brilliant, others really cared about me. A good teacher can make the difference in whether or not you really learn anything.

In college I was once assigned to write a term paper on a topic I knew nothing about—Islamic eschatology. The day before my paper was due, I brought my work to a professor who was an expert in Islam. I remember the confused look on his face as he read. It turns out my sources had included someone who is considered a radical in the Muslim world.

I was sunk. The paper was worth 40 percent of my grade. To my surprise, this professor picked up his phone and informed his wife that he would not be home for supper. He stayed with me until 9:00 that night in the library, helping me find more reliable resources for my paper. I stayed up all night and handed the paper in the next morning. While it was the quickest paper I had ever written, I was confident it was good, because this time I had a good teacher supervising my work.

We have learned that we interpret Scripture whenever we read it. And yet the greatest theologians of all times have wrestled with Scripture and failed to agree on their interpretation. If they struggle, then how can ordinary followers of Jesus ever hope to understand it?

The easy answer is . . . because you have a good teacher. As you read Scripture, the Holy Spirit is your guide and interpreter. The verse printed at the beginning of this reading says that the Holy Spirit will teach us what we need to know.

Often people are intimidated by Scripture, and rightfully so. It can be hard, if not impossible, to understand. Education helps. So does understanding the historical context and genre of a particular Scripture passage. But remember, our goal is not so much trying to understand the Bible as it is trying to understand God. And no one—whether you've dropped out of high school or earned a string of advanced degrees—can understand God, at least not without divine aid.

From Solomon in the Old Testament to Jesus' brother James in the New Testament, Scripture consistently states that true wisdom is not earned. It is a gift from God.

How does the Spirit work? God appears to use his Spirit in a number of ways.

- Jesus says that the Holy Spirit will "guide you into all the truth" (John 16:12). It is comforting to know that when we read Scripture, *its author is present* with us, guiding us in truth. That reminds us that Scripture is personal. It's not a set of abstract doctrinal propositions. In its pages God personally reveals himself and personally addresses us in our own circumstances. It is God's Word revealing God's word.

- The Holy Spirit also works *in community.* God has placed us in a church that can help us interpret Scripture. This community of interpretation not only exists now, but it stretches back into the early church. For every part of Scripture, there's a long tradition of interpretation. That tradition does not end the discussion, but that's where it ought to begin. The Holy Spirit works within the body of Christ or the church to help interpret the Bible.

- The Holy Spirit also works through *preparation.* The gift of the Holy Spirit is not a license for laziness. God's presence is with you in your day-to-day reading of Scripture as well as other works that are meant to help your understanding of Scripture.

Because of sin (Rom. 1:21) no one is able to understand God's Word without divine aid. But praise God for the Spirit who enables us to read and understand God's Word and catch a glimpse of the One who wrote it!

I was blessed to have a professor who was an expert in his field take the time to guide me in my research. We are even more blessed to have God as our divine guide in revealing the truths contained in his Word.

Think It Over

When have you experienced God speaking personally to you while reading or listening to the Bible? Reflect on the experience. What were the circumstances in your life, or ways in which you approached the Scripture, that made it more possible for God to speak?

In Other Words

"It is entirely possible to come to the Bible in total sincerity, responding to the intellectual challenges it gives, or for the moral guidance it offers, or for the spiritual uplift it provides, and not . . . deal with a personally revealing God who has personal designs on you."

—Eugene Peterson, *Eat This Book*

Live It Out

Not just today, but every time before you read God's Word, ask for the Holy Spirit to come and speak to you personally as your guide and teacher.

Meditation 4

"Oh, how I love your law! I meditate on it all day long. Your commands are always with me and make me wiser than my enemies. I have more insight than all my teachers, for I meditate on your statutes."

—Psalm 119:97-99

One day in college a friend of mine invited me to hike a twenty-five-mile section of the North Country Trail in Michigan. This was an ambitious goal, but we were both in good physical shape. We awoke early in the morning on the appointed day, drove a couple of hours to the trailhead, and laced up our boots. From the very first step I had only one goal in mind—to finish. I was pushing the pace, making great time and encouraging my friend to keep up.

After a while I got a little frustrated at the slow pace of my partner. When we stopped for a break after an hour or so, he was excited. "Did you see all those deer?" he asked. "No," I replied. Did you see that beautiful oriole?" I hadn't seen that either.

We were walking a beautiful trail surrounded by God's glorious creation, and I saw nothing. I was so focused on the destination that I missed the excitement of the journey. From then on I walked slower, looked more, and tried to take everything in.

The same can be said about the Bible. Sometimes I simply read the Bible in order to get done. I do my devotions so that I can finish them and maybe feel a little better about myself. I have read the Bible in a year more than once, and on many days the task felt like nothing more than an assignment. Each day I could check off my reading as another task completed.

Mind you, there's nothing wrong with simply reading Scripture. And reading the Bible in one or three years is a noble goal. But the psalmist reminds us that there is a difference between *reading* the Bible and *studying* or *meditating* on it.

Whether you read the Bible once or a thousand times, if you do not understand what you read, then you have not achieved the ultimate goal of loving and knowing God better through his Word.

Reading the Bible is not a race. There are no extra rewards in heaven for those who have read it the most or the fastest. The quality of our reading is more important than the quantity.

The psalmist says he meditates on God's Word day and night. *Meditating* on Scripture usually means reading it carefully or even memorizing it. The Hebrew word is related to the way a cow chews the cud. Scripture gets chewed, masticated, swallowed, and brought up again. That way, every rich enzyme of truth, every nutrient-laden personal vitamin gets processed. If you take the time to *study* Scripture, not just read it, but really study, memorize, and "chew" on it, then God's Word will continue to shape all aspects of your life.

Once again, we turn to the example of Jesus' temptation by Satan in the wilderness in Luke 4. On three different occasions Satan approaches Jesus with tempting offers. All three times, Jesus rebukes Satan by using Scripture. Jesus knew the book of Deuteronomy by heart, so when Satan attacked him he was ready with a biblical defense he could recall from memory.

Jesus had internalized the word of God. He had let it become part of how he thought and acted. Jesus says that the Holy Spirit will help us recall what we have learned as well (John 14:26). The Spirit will not magically put biblical words in our minds or mouths that we have never bothered to learn. Rather, God will help us recall what we have studied and meditated upon.

At the encouragement of my spiritual mentor, I have memorized significant passages of the New Testament. Memorizing for me is not easy: I have to read, re-read, and read again until I finally remember it. As a pastor there have been numerous times when God's Word provided me with answers in a ministry situation.

The Bible is not a novel. Its pages include more than a hundred lifetimes of material to be studied. I encourage you to read the Bible carefully. Read it deliberately. And read it prayerfully. As you read, try to understand what God is saying to you.

Think It Over

1. How often do you read the Bible like a hurried hiker who is so focused on the destination that he doesn't see the beauty around him? How can you slow down?

2. Have you memorized any parts of the Bible, perhaps as a child? When and how do these words come back to you?

In Other Words

"Reading is an immense gift, but only if the words are assimilated, taken into the soul—eaten, chewed, gnawed, received in unhurried delight."

—Eugene Peterson, *Eat This Book*

Live It Out

Memorize Psalm 103 or a passage of your choice. Meditate on what it means for your life.

Read and Obey 5

"Therefore everyone who hears these words of mine and puts them into practice is like a wise man who built his house on the rock."

—Matthew 7:24

Some words are meant to entertain, others to enlighten. Some words are meant to be obeyed. Let's say someone yells, "Get out of the way—that truck lost its brakes!" Those words are not meant to be analyzed or diagrammed into subject, object, and verb. They are not a thing of beauty to be savored. They are simply meant to be obeyed.

Jesus points to one of the keys to reading the Bible. It's God's Word, and it's meant to be put into practice. We can savor its beauty, reflect on its stories, investigate its deep theological truths. But at heart God's Word is meant to be practiced, obeyed, lived.

Eugene Peterson, who I've quoted a lot, is a linguist and biblical scholar. He's also the translator who has given us *The Message,* an immensely popular modern paraphrase that has brought the Bible to life for millions of people. He's obviously thought a lot about what the Bible says and how we relate to it.

In *Eat This Book,* Peterson describes how he once took up running again after a few years of neglect. He was soon competing in 10K races and even an annual marathon. He subscribed to a number of running magazines and checked out books on running from the library. He enjoyed reading about diet, stretching exercises, resting heart rate, electrolyte replacements, and all the techniques designed to make him a more efficient runner.

Then he pulled a muscle. His doctor told him that he had to stop running for a couple of months to give the muscle a rest. He writes, "It took me about two weeks to notice that since my injury I hadn't picked up a running book or opened a running magazine. I didn't *decide* not to read them; they were still all over the house, but I wasn't reading them. I wasn't reading because I wasn't running. The moment I began running I started reading again" (pp. 70-71).

That's the primary way we read the Bible. If we're not running the race of discipleship, if we're not seeking to live in Christ, then the Bible doesn't make much sense and we're likely to neglect it. In fact, this may be one of the chief indicators for us of how serious we are about being disciples of Jesus. The Bible is our running magazine, and we'll only have a passion to read it if we're in the race.

Peterson says, "The parallel with reading Scripture seems to me almost exact: if I am not participating in the reality—the God reality, the creation/salvation/holiness reality—revealed in the Bible, not involved in the obedience Calvin wrote of, I am probably not going to be much interested in reading about it, at least not for long" (p. 71).

Obedience, then, is the place where reading the Bible and discipleship meet.

Now *obedience* is a hard word, and maybe it's not the best word. It works when there's an emergency, like a warning that a truck with no brakes is bearing down on you. I need to hear the Bible's commands when I'm straying from the path of discipleship. Watch what you say! Be careful about how you relate to money! Keep sex within the covenant relationship of love!

But it's more than obedience. It's also *practice*.

When we're reading about running or golf or cooking or home maintenance, it's not just a matter of obedience. Yes, there may be certain rules to follow, certain pitfalls to avoid. But the heart of it is the desire to master this game, this skill, this situation in life. It's not so much obeying commands as being part of a community that loves this thing and wants to practice it as best they can.

So we read the Bible as part of a community that wants to practice living in the reality of God's kingdom. That means watching out for the pitfalls of personal sin, caring for creation, being passionate about justice, and wanting to know all I can about the God I love and worship.

Still, when reading the Bible, our first response is not "What does this mean?" or "Isn't that interesting?" but "How can I obey?" "A simple act of obedience," says Peterson, "will open up our lives to this text far more quickly than any number of Bible studies and dictionaries and concordances" (p. 71).

Think It Over

1. How has your own experience shown that your desire to read the Bible is related to your commitment to live by it?

2. What barriers, if any, stand in the way of your regular Bible reading?

In Other Words

"All right knowledge of God is born of obedience."

—John Calvin, *Institutes of the Christian Religion,* 1.6.2

Live It Out

Read Matthew 7:24-27 and write down or illustrate those parts of your life that are being built on the rock and on the sand.

Digging In
Discussion Guide

In Acts 8:26-35, Luke tells the story of an Ethiopian government official who had made a visit to Jerusalem and was on his way home. Evidently he was intrigued by the Hebrew Scripture and wanted to understand it better. By a special act of the Holy Spirit, a Christian named Philip met him on the road. Seeing the man reading the scroll of Isaiah, Philip asked, "Do you understand what you are reading?" The man answered, "How can I unless someone explains it to me?"

There are rare stories of people coming to faith in Christ by just reading the Bible on their own. But let's face it, the Bible is not an easy book to read and understand. When you start reading in the middle of the story somewhere, you can get lost. The Ethiopian was reading from Isaiah, which prophesies the coming death of Christ, but he couldn't get it unless someone explained the connection. "'Who is the prophet talking about, himself or someone else?' Then Philip began with that very passage of Scripture and told him the good news about Jesus."

This week we will discuss ways in which we can better understand and interpret the Bible, both for ourselves and for others God may place in our path, like the Ethiopian. We will also be in a better position to judge the interpretations of others, which is always necessary in our religiously diverse society.

For Starters

(10 minutes)

Invite each person in the group to mention one helpful thought, inspirational insight, or question that arose from the daily readings. Don't have a discussion yet, just listen as people share their thoughts.

Let's Focus

(5 minutes)

Read the introduction to this session (if you haven't already) and then have someone read this focus statement aloud.

The Bible is not the kind of easy read you might pick up for mind-numbing entertainment. It comes to us out of other cultures and languages. It is complex and many-faceted, and it includes a variety of types of literature. Over the centuries Christians have developed methods and strategies of interpretation and understanding that have stood the test of time. Still, as difficult as it may sometimes seem, countless people continue to experience it directly as God's Word for their lives. It's the book that understands them.

Word Search

(20 minutes)

Read aloud the following Scripture passages and briefly discuss at least some of the questions under each one (or formulate your own questions).

- Read Psalm 119:89-112

  Known as the longest psalm and the longest chapter in the Bible, Psalm 119 is a beautiful reflection on the importance of Scripture. What are some of the different terms used for Scripture here?

  What are some of the metaphors used to describe how the writer/ poet relates to Scripture? Which is your favorite?

- Read Luke 4:1-13
  In this passage Jesus is tempted by the devil. Notice that Jesus responds to each of the devil's attacks with a quotation from Scripture (Deut. 8:3; 6:13; and 6:16). How do you think Jesus knew these Scriptures? Looking at their context, what do you notice about how Jesus interpreted and applied these texts? Invite group members to share a time in their lives when Scripture helped them deal with temptation.

> **In Other Words**
>
> "Judaism openly espouses a kind of concentric-circle view of authority: the Ten Commandments at the very center, then the mitzvoth (the rest of the ancient code of Jewish law), then the whole Torah (all of Genesis through Deuteronomy), then the books of the prophets, then the Writings . . . then the Talmud (commentary from early centuries), then Midrash (more commentary on the Talmud)."
>
> —Debra Rienstra, *So Much More*

Bring It Home
(15 minutes)

Choose one of the following options:

Option 1
Having read a part of Psalm 119, work together as a group to compose a few verses of your own psalm praising God's Word. You might begin by thinking of some new metaphors for reading and understanding the Bible and some new ways of expressing its importance in your life. Work together to compose a few verses of your own psalm out of these ideas. Write them on a board or on newsprint.

Option 2
Discuss *some* of these questions as time allows, or discuss a problem or question group members highlighted earlier from the daily readings.

- Identify and discuss some of the misuses or misinterpretations of the Bible you have observed.

- There seems to be a growing ignorance of the Bible today, even among Christians. Discuss why this might be and what can be done to combat it.

- What is the biggest problem you have in reading the Bible? What is your biggest joy in reading it? Discuss these together as time allows.

Option 3

Working on your own, write down a brief plan for how you will integrate reading the Bible more fully into your daily life. (For example, begin a read-the-Bible-in-a year plan, participate in a group Bible study, memorization, and the like.) Share your plan with the group.

Pray It Through

(10 minutes)

As you come to the end of this study, pray for each group member. (One way to do this is for each member to pray for the person on the right or left.)

- Pray for the problems that have been expressed or commitments made in the group.

- Pray that God will continue to reveal himself to each person through Scripture.

- Pray for discipline to read and the wisdom to interpret the most important book ever written.

- Pray that the Holy Spirit will continue to change each person's life as he or she obediently reads God's Word.

- Pray that God will use each person to help others (family, friends, interested non-Christians) to love and understand the Bible as Philip did.

Live It Out

If you haven't already done so, write down a plan to integrate Bible reading more fully into your daily life (begin a read-the-Bible-in-a year plan, join a group Bible study, or memorize Scripture, for example). If you have already done this in the group, refine the plan and begin to put it into practice.

---(Web Alert)---

Be sure to check out the participants' section for this session on www.GrowDisciples.org for interesting links and suggestions for readings and activities that will deepen your understanding of the Bible.